Ibiza
Form

CW00369425

- A ☞ in the text denotes a highly recommended sight
- A complete A–Z of practical information starts on p.99
- Extensive mapping on cover flaps

Berlitz Publishing Company, Inc.

Princeton   Mexico City   Dublin   Eschborn   Singapore

Copyright © **1998**, 1996 by Berlitz Publishing Co., Inc.
400 Alexander Park, Princeton, NJ, 08540 USA
9-13 Grosvenor St., London, W1X 9FB UK

All rights reserved. No part of this book may be reproduced or transmitted in any form or by any means, electronic or mechanical, including photocopying, recording or by any information storage and retrieval system without permission in writing from the publisher.

Berlitz Trademark Reg. U.S. Patent Office and other countries
Marca Registrada

Text:	Ken Bernstein, Norman Renouf
Editors:	Donald Greig, Renée Ferguson
Photography:	Jon Davison, Neil Wilson
Cover photo:	© Tom Craig/FPG International
Layout:	Media Content Marketing, Inc.
Cartography:	Falk-Verlag, Munich

Thanks to Spanish National Tourist office for their invaluable help in the preparation of this guide.

Found an error we should know about? Our editor would be happy to hear from you, and a postcard would do. Although we make every effort to ensure the accuracy of all the information in this book, changes do occur.

ISBN 2-8315-6421-2
Revised 1998 – Second Printing July 1998

Printed in Switzerland by Weber SA, Bienne
029/807 RP

CONTENTS

IBIZA

IBIZA AND FORMENTERA

Ibiza offers a healthy slice of the Mediterranean lifestyle infused with some of the spirit and architecture of North Africa. Although it is strictly a part of the Spanish archipelago known as the *Islas Pitiusas*, or pine-covered isles, Ibiza in fact displays many of the characteristics of the *Islas Baleares*, or Balearic Islands, of neighbouring Mallorca and Menorca, with which it is commonly grouped. In terms of government, it is part of the Spanish province of Baleares. Here you'll find all the resorts, bars, and discos you could wish for, but there are also traditional villages, deserted beaches, secret coves, and quiet walks for when all you want to do is escape the fray.

Formentera, Ibiza's diminutive neighbour just one hour's ferry-boat ride (or 25 minutes by hydrofoil) to the south, is an island apart—in some ways more like a desert island than a satellite or outpost of Ibiza. During the supremacy of the Barbary Coast pirates in the 16th and 17th centuries, Formentera was so vulnerable it had to be abandoned, and it wasn't resettled until the 18th century. Now it offers the perfect antidote to the stress of modern-day living, and is the ideal place to recharge yourself before another evening of exuberant nightlife back on "mainland" Ibiza. Alternatively, if you prefer to find an even quieter stretch of beach, the waters around Ibiza are dotted with a host of minor islets, most uninhabited but all eminently explorable.

One thing you'll quickly realize about Ibiza is its *laissez-faire* attitude towards life. On this island paradise, tourists and expatriates coexist side by side with movie stars, artists, the young and trendy, ageing hippies, and, of course, locals, the total residential population being over 80,000. Despite the onset of tourism, in many parts the islanders still adhere to old traditions, living off the fruits (literally!) of land and sea. Ibiza, small as it is, is *not* one of those barren Mediterranean rocks with an allure that begins and ends at the beach, and although it's a part of Spain, it is *not* the usual bullfight-and-flamenco scene. The people are a distinct race: they have a unique, ancient heritage and a passionate folklore all their own. They also have their own language, Ibicenco, a dialect related to the *mallorquí* (Majorcan) branch of the Catalan language, though Castilian is spoken as well.

Finding Your Way

Ibicenco, the dialect often spoken by islanders among themselves, is closely related to Catalan and sounds rather like Portuguese. Its roots are Latin, and its vocabulary is spiced with Arabic ingredients. On Ibiza and Formentera some place names are in Ibicenco, while others are in Castilian. The Ibicenco name for Ibiza is Eivissa.

The following list of common Castilian and Ibicenco words should help to keep you on the right track.

English	Castilian/Ibicenco	English	Castilian/Ibicenco
avenue	avenida/avinguda or vía/via	fountain	fuente/font
		harbour	puerto/port
beach	playa/platja	quarter	barrio/barri
boulevard	paseo/passeig	river	río/riu
bridge	puente/pont	road	carretera/carretera
bullring	plaza de toros/ plaça de braus or de toros		
		square	plaza/plaça
		street	calle/carrer
cape	cabo/cap	town hall	ayuntamiento/ ajuntament
cave	cueva/cova		
church	iglesia/església		

Ibiza lies nearer to the coast of North Africa than to the Catalonian city of Barcelona. With an area of just 541 sq km (209 sq miles), it is slightly smaller than the Isle of Man or twice Martha's Vineyard in Massachusetts. It may not be much of a speck on the globe, but it is big enough to contain a modest mountain, verdant farms, and —that real Mediterranean novelty—a river. Likewise, the island's highest peak, Mount Sa Talaia, or Atalaya (475 meters/1,558 feet), hardly ranks among the world's most dramatic, but you can see Spain from the top.

Agriculture is a way of life for a large number of Ibiza's inhabitants.

The climate here is distinctly Mediterranean: temperature extremes are uncommon and days are warm throughout the year, with the heat of the summer usually tempered by sea breezes. This, combined with the island's extraordinary underground water resources, assures the success of Ibiza's agriculture. For the tourist, the olive, fig, and almond trees are objects of beauty and colour; for the farmer, they're cash crops. So is the salt, drying in the huge, square pans at Las Salinas in the south.

The capital of Ibiza, called simply Ibiza, or Ibiza Town, has a population of almost 35,000. This is the island's main city and financial, governmental, and administrative centre, and its charms match those of other Mediterranean "jewels."

From the pine-clad hills of Ibiza (above) to Es Pujols on Formentera (right), peaceful natural beauty abounds.

It is also a major entertainment spot with its own appeal, from the whitewashed houses of the ancient walled city clambering up the hillside to the hustle and bustle of the harbour area, with its bistros and boutiques. Its popularity is such that it has gained a reputation for being something of a trend-setters' haven—post-modern or New Age, this is the place to be.

The busiest tourist town on the island lies 15 km (9 miles) west of the capital. The Romans called it *Portus Magnus* (great port), which the Ibicencos adapted to *Portmany*. You might still come across both versions, but the official name of the boom town is Sant Antoni Abad (San Antonio in Castilian or Abbot St. Anthony in English). Skirting the bay, which has been transformed into a variation on Rio de Janeiro's Copacabana Beach, are high-rise hotels and apartment buildings. The resort is a centre not only for beach activities but for lively nightlife as well.

The second largest—as opposed to busiest—town on the island is Santa Eulària del Riu (or Río) on the east coast. Originally this was merely a hamlet on a hilltop crowned by a picturesque fortress-church. Now the tourist imperative has extended the town all the way down to the sea and far along the coast.

Other villages are much less developed, and therein lies the essence of many delights. If you head inland to the less populous centre of the island, you'll find hamlets consisting of little more than a whitewashed church, a general store, and a bar. This is the time to relax over a glass of the locally made *hierbas* (an alcoholic drink made from herbs), listen to the crickets, and watch the world go by.

A BRIEF HISTORY

A handful of Bronze Age relics has fostered an assumption that prehistoric settlers inhabited Ibiza thousands of years ago. Greater evidence of such a people is found on Mallorca and Menorca than on Ibiza, but one of the Balearics' most important sites is actually on the island of Formentera, where the megalithic monument/tomb of Ca Na Costa has been dated to 2000 B.C.

Ibiza's key location between Africa and ancient Iberia made it a convenient stopover for Mediterranean seafarers, such as the Phoenician traders, who called the island Ibosim. The Greeks dubbed it Ebysos, the Romans called it Ebusus, and the Moors, Yebisah.

Puig des Molins

Apart from its funerary function, the Carthaginian necropolis of Puig des Molins below Ibiza Town's Dalt Vila may well have been the scene of infant sacrifice. Archaeologists have established that at a pottery nearby, in what is now Via Romana, terra-cotta figures of gods and goddesses were made. These statuettes probably represent deities who were believed to protect the dead in the next world. Of special significance for the Carthaginians were both Tanit, goddess of the underworld, and her consort, Baal.

In the Punic colony, craftsmen created figurines of animals which were associated with Tanit (the lion) and Baal (the bull) and clay plaques which bore the image of death as a horseman, or various life-and-resurrection symbols, especially palm branches, lotus flowers, and the crescent moon. These pieces, which were striking in their simplicity, follow North African prototypes. They are coarse and unsophisticated—obviously made for a people whose business instincts were more highly developed than their esthetic sensibilities.

Ca Na Costa remains on Formentera as a monument to the island's prehistoric inhabitants.

The Carthaginians

A detailed history of the island doesn't begin until it became a colony of Carthage in the 7th century B.C. (see also pages 14-15). The Carthaginians originally came from the area comprising present-day Lebanon, and from their bases in North Africa and what's now Spain, they challenged the Roman Empire for domination of the Mediterranean region. Their interest in Ibiza lay partly in its vast salt flats, which to this day remain the source of a profitable industry. They capitalized on the natural resources by using the salt to cure fish, which they exported to their home country. The Carthaginians also carried out lead mining and continued to be of significance up until this century. It is believed that the lead pellets which were used by the Carthaginian general Hannibal were made on Ibiza.

IBIZA, COLONY OF CARTHAGE

Believing that its clay could repel animals and harmful substances, the Carthaginians considered Ibiza a holy island, and claimed it in the seventh century B.C. From the time of its colonization by the North African nation, the island steadily grew in importance, and for centuries it ranked as one of the major commercial and military centres in the Mediterranean. Decline set in with the defeat of Carthage by the Romans (146 B.C.), yet Ibiza held fast to the fierce gods and gory customs of the Punic past, preserving the traditions of Carthage long into the Roman period.

Archaeologists paint a fascinating picture of life, death, and ritual in the Punic colony. More than 20 ancient sites—necropolises or vast cities of the dead, and religious shrines—have been explored since the turn of the century, and a wealth of objects has come to light. The most important necropolis, at Puig des Molins, boasts some 4,000 tombs, though fewer than 300 have actually been uncovered. Here you can see the spacious burial chambers constructed for rich citizens of the Punic capital. They were laid to rest in enormous stone sarcophagi, sur-

rounded by the paraphernalia of a happy afterlife: unguent jars, lanterns, terra-cotta statuettes of deities, ostrich eggs decorated with symbols of life and resurrection. The less affluent made do with a shallow tomb or simple sarcophagus set into the hillside. Cheaper still, if less roomy, was an ordinary amphora just large enough to hold the ashes of the departed.

Other important Punic sites include the sanctuaries of Isla Plana, a little peninsula jutting into the Bahía d'Ibiza, and Es

Cuieram, a cave near Sant Vicenç in the sparsely populated northeastern quadrant of the island. From the earliest period of Carthaginian colonization, Isla Plana was a holy place. People came here to seek protection from evil in general, difficulties in childbirth and childhood illnesses in particular, and even from death itself. Es Cuieram was dedicated to the cult of Tanit, at its peak from the fourth to the second centuries B.C. The isolation of the cave did not stop believers from depositing gold medallions and hundreds of terra-cotta figures here. Oddly, nearly all the terra cottas were blackened by fire; this, together with the quantities of bones and ashes uncovered in the cave, points to the performance of some kind of funerary rite at Es Cuieram.

For all its vitality, Punic culture died out. By the close of the Roman era, Es Cuieram, Isla Plana, Puig des Molins, and Ibiza's other sanctuaries and necropolises lay abandoned and forgotten. But not for long. After the Arab conquest in the ninth–tenth centuries, thieves plundered the tombs of Puig des Molins, stripping them of precious gold jewellery. To complete the archaeological record, they left behind the lamps that lighted up their search.

Sadly, the plunder continued earlier this century, when unscrupulous archaeologists formed private collections of Punic art and artefacts in the course of "official" excavations. There were plenty of clandestine digs, too. One antiques dealer from Mallorca kept a legion of islanders on the lookout for additions to his collection. He later exhibited the finds in Barcelona, pocketing the proceeds. Not long afterwards, Barcelona's archaeological museum acquired every last object for a handsome sum.

Although many key pieces of Punic art have been dispersed or lost, many more are on display in Ibiza's archaeological museums. Gold work, jewellery, the painted spheres of ostrich eggs, and exquisitely modelled terra-cottas all provide valuable insight into the island's past. These objects of ritual and ornamentation perplex and intrigue; above all, however, they sum up as nothing else can the spirit of Carthage itself.

The Carthaginians also considered the island a holy place, and here in great splendour they buried thousands of their citizens in a huge necropolis on the Puig des Molins (Hill of the Windmills) below the Dalt Vila (Old Town) of Ibiza. Under the gnarled olive trees archaeologists have uncovered a treasure trove of statues, jewellery, pitchers, tools, and coins, which are now displayed in the town's two archaeological museums.

The church of Santa Eulària del Riu (above), and the museum at Sant Fancesc Xavier (opposite).

The Romans

The Romans never really infiltrated Ibiza, and even after the defeat of Hannibal in 202 B.C. during the Second Punic War their influence was restrained. Only with the fall of Carthage in 146 B.C. did they manage to make inroads, but, as local historians stress, Ibiza was neither conquered nor annexed by Rome, but confederated, retaining remarkable autonomy. For centuries to come the old Carthaginian traditions were allowed to continue on Ibiza alongside the new Roman way of life. Meanwhile on the Iberian peninsula, Rome was leaving a decisive imprint on the area's language, culture, and government, and particularly in its engineering genius in the construction of roads, aqueducts, and monuments.

The Romans also exploited Ibiza's natural resources. They exported salt from the southern end of the island and lead from the mines of Sant Carles, and at the same time extracted a purple dye from shellfish which was used for imperial cloaks. In addition they found a moneymaker in an exotic, aromatic sauce of decomposed fish innards. Called *garum*, it was considered a great delicacy by Romans and Greeks alike. (Today it is but a historical footnote; local cooks use nothing more pungent than a hint of garlic.)

The Moors

After centuries of peace and productivity, the year A.D. 426 marked the beginning of an era of strife, violence, and destruction. Ibiza, along with the rest of what is now Spain, was invaded and sacked by the Germanic tribe of the Vandals, who

occupied the island and quickly imposed their culture. Centuries of almost constant repressive foreign rule followed, with the Vandals being succeeded by the Byzantines, Saracens, and Moors.

The Moorish conquest of the Balearics was complete by A.D. 903, and except during the periodic outbreaks of violence typical of that time, the Moors devoted themselves to developing the island economy and agriculture. However, little evidence remains of that era —some ceramics in the museum, a few fortifications, a network of irrigation ditches. For the most part, the Moorish legacy is manifested in a few local place

The Portal de Las Tablas marks the entrance to the walled city, Dalt Vila, the old town of Ibiza.

names, some words in the Ibicenco dialect, and an indelible influence on the island's folk music. Indeed, perhaps the most vivid reminder of the Moors are the dark, brooding eyes of so many of the islanders of today.

Christian Reconquest

The Moors were determined to carry Islam into Europe. To this end they invaded Spain itself and even reached up into France until they were beaten by the Frankish ruler Charles Martel in 732. But after the Crusade of Pisa (see page 19), Islamic power waned, and in the early 13th century Ibiza was embraced by the Christian Reconquest. King James I of Aragon authorized the occupation of the islands under forces commanded by Guillermo de Montgri, a solid Catalonian citizen with titular ecclesiastical rank. After a few skirmishes, the Catalonian troops were ready to deal the death blow. One pincer battered its way through the rebuilt city wall, while the other—so it is said—infiltrated through a secret passage revealed to the invaders by the brother of the sheik himself. According to legend the embittered traitor gave the game away because the passionate sheik had seduced his wife.

Thus, violently, in August 1235, both Christianity and the Catalonian language came to Ibiza to stay. On the mainland, the *Reconquista* (Reconquest) continued for another two and one-half centuries. The Moors suffered a major setback in 1212 at the battle of Navas de Tolosa in northern Andalusia, but they still clung to the kingdom of Granada and were only finally evicted from there in 1492.

The Crusade of Pisa

One event during Moorish times in Ibiza lives in local legend. The island was on the receiving end of the ministrations of Pope Paschal II who, to cleanse the Mediterranean of infidels and pirates, mounted what was called the Crusade of Pisa in 1113. Ibiza was a likely target, but who would have expected all 500 warships of the crusade's fleet to turn up at the island? The ensuing offensive turned into weeks of siege.

The islanders put up a particularly gallant show. They rallied round the Moorish viceroy, Abdul-Manzor, to repel one bloody charge after another. Finally, however, the besieged Ibicencos persuaded their leader to admit that the day was lost and hoist the white flag. The pious Pisans punished the bloodied islanders, dismantled what remained of the battered city wall, and hauled away all the booty they could grab.

Booty and Plunder

Elsewhere, great events were changing the shape of the world. Under Ferdinand and Isabella, the unity of Spain as the country we know today was finally achieved, and it was carrying their flag that in 1492 Christopher Columbus sailed westwards and discovered America. Soon Spain found itself the recipient of immense wealth in the form of gold and silver, and the Spanish rulers, eager for more, turned their attention away from the Mediterranean and Ibiza towards both the New World and the heart of Europe, where Spanish ambitions rapidly expanded. Ibiza became a mere backwater, largely forgotten but for shipwreck or plague.

The moment that the Spanish monarchs looked the other way, the daring pirates of the North African Barbary Coast —and elsewhere—moved in. The Ibicencos fortified the bulwarks and built additional towers and fortresses throughout to help shield themselves against enemy incursions. Despite their efforts, however, Ibiza was menaced by so many hostile flotillas that the locals took the unprecedented step of forming their own band of privateers. To the Berbers' amazement the tables were turned, and it wasn't long before the Ibicencos were boarding the enemy's brigantines on the open seas and "liberating" the pirates' booty— even that of the greatly feared "Pope" (see box). Today an obelisk in

The Pope

According to local tradition, the most villainous foreign swashbuckler of all was a pirate from Gibraltar, Captain Miguel Novelli, alias The Pope. When he sailed to attack Ibiza in his, the *Felicity*, he was confronted by a local captain, Antonio Riquer, midway between Ibiza and Formentera. Although Riquer had only eight guns compared to The Pope's dozen cannons, the local boy made good.

Ibiza's port honours the daring Corsairs.

Reminders of the permanent threat posed by pirates can be found everywhere on Ibiza. In the towns it is notable that the churches and other focal points from that period were built on an elevated site to provide lookout posts and early warning systems. In many isolated regions, meanwhile, lastditch defences in the form of round stone towers were built, a few of which are still inhabited today. An unusual collection of such towers can be seen from the Sant Joan road in a hamlet with the Moorish name of Balafi, near the village of Sant Lorenç.

The Corsair Obelisk (Obelisco a los Corsarios) is believed to be the world's only monument in praise of privateers.

Political Turmoil

In the 19th and early 20th centuries, Spain was both economically weak and politically unstable. It lost its empire in America and the Pacific, and then in 1923 suffered a humiliating defeat in Morocco at the hands of local rebels. Under King Alfonso XIII neither dictatorship nor constitutional government was able to create and sustain domestic tranquillity, with the result that following anti-royalist election results in 1931 the king went into exile.

Structures built as look-out posts are visible throughout Ibiza's Old Quarter.

The turbulence continued under the new republic continued to be turbulent, however, with bitter ideological divisions between parties and factions, involving the church as well. Finally, in 1936, a large section of the army under General Francisco Franco rose in revolt, claiming the support of the monarchists, conservatives, the Church, and the right-wing Falange party, the fascist movement which had been founded in 1933 and which Franco subsequently declared to be the only legal party in Spain. Opposing him was a collection of republicans, liberals, socialists, communists, and anarchists.

The Spanish Civil War became one of the *causes célèbres* of the 20th century, with support for both sides being rallied in many countries outside Spain. In Ibiza several families were torn in their loyalties between the Republican and Nationalist causes. The bloodshed lasted three years and cost hundreds of thousands of lives, and almost every family on Ibiza—not to mention the mainland—was touched by tragedy. Ibiza, Formentera, and Menorca were all captured by loyalist forces, who used the islands as a base for their naval operations. Hardship was compounded with the advent of World War II, even though Spain stayed neutral throughout the war.

HISTORICAL LANDMARKS

c.2000 B.C.	Bronze Age peoples inhabit the Balearic Islands.
600 B.C.	Carthaginians colonize Ibiza.
218–201 B.C.	Second Punic War; Carthaginian General Hannibal defeated in 202 B.C.
146 B.C.	Fall of Carthage to the Romans.
123 B.C.	Ibiza confederated by Rome.
A.D. 426	Ibiza raided and sacked by Vandals.
A.D. 903	Moorish conquest of Balearics complete.
1235	Reconquista (Reconquest) of Ibiza; Christianity restored.
1469	Ferdinand II of Aragon marries Isabella of Castile, uniting the crowns of Aragon and Castile. Spain becomes a Mediterranean power and the Balearics important strategic posts.
1492	Christopher Columbus discovers America.
1500	Balearics decline in importance; start of the Barbary Coast pirate raids.
1662	Ibiza scourged by the plague, population falls.
1799–1815	Napoleonic Wars lead to stronger European presence in the Mediterranean and end pirate raids from North Africa.
1931	King Alfonso XIII of Spain goes into exile.
1936	Rise of General Franco and the Falange Party.
1936–1938	Spanish Civil War; Ibiza captured by loyalist forces.
1939–1945	World War II; Spain remains nominally neutral.
1960s	The introduction of wide-bodied jets prompts the development of mass tourism. Ibiza inundated with foreign visitors.
1975	Death of Franco, restoration of the Spanish monarchy.
1981	King Juan Carlos I thwarts a military coup.
1982	Felipe González and socialist government elected.
1986	Spain admitted to the European Union (then "Community").

The shattered Spanish economy inched forward during the post-war years. For Ibiza the breakthrough came in the 1960s, with the introduction of wide-bodied jets and a significant surge in tourism. Following the expansion of the airport, the island entered the big league of international holiday resorts.

After the death of Franco in 1975, King Juan Carlos I restored democracy to Spain. In free elections in June 1977, moderates and democratic socialists emerged as the largest parties. Ibiza's new freedom meant the renaissance of the Ibicenco language and culture after decades of suppression, and participation in Catalonia's newly won autonomy. Free speech and free elections were not the only innovations: gambling was legalized and nude bathing was sanctioned. Change swept through Ibiza dramatically, irrevocably, almost overnight.

Take a break from the beach and explore the rich history of Ibiza through its architectural relics.

Modern Times

Since then, the development of Ibiza has continued, and the island's fortunes are now almost completely derived from tourism. Changes on mainland Spain have inevitably been felt on Ibiza also, but their effect has been

The fountains of Ibiza's Parc de la Reina Sofia, a symbol of today's Spanish monarchy.

largely beneficial. The Socialist Workers' Party of Felipe González Márquez was elected in 1982 and his government committed itself to Spain's integration into the European Union (formerly the European Community). As a precondition to admission, the border with Gibraltar was reopened in 1985 after a 16-year hiatus, and Spain was admitted to the EU in 1986. In spite of high unemployment and separatist rumblings, the country's economic growth rate remained one of the highest in all of western Europe throughout the 1980s. Although Ibiza's popularity as a holiday destination has never waned, the events of the past few years—Seville Expo '92, the Barcelona Olympics—have ensured its continued success.

WHERE TO GO

IBIZA

From architecture to zoology, Ibiza—laid back, yet lively —offers things seen nowhere else on earth. Whether your interests are as serious as ancient history or as energetic as windsurfing, you'll find new stimulation on *la Isla Blanca*— the White Island, as this destination is often called because of its white houses.

Each area of the island offers something different. The Sa Penya and Dalt Vila districts of Ibiza Town have lots of trendy boutiques, Santa Eulària boasts some of the island's best restaurants, while Sant Antoni is notorious for its discos and bars. You'll also want to discover the "real" Ibiza —the country of farmers and fishermen. All you need to do is just wander off the beaten path, beyond the bustling tourist zone.

If you crave a change of environment, a day's outing to Formentera offers the bonus of a sea voyage. Life is simpler on this secluded island and the beaches are not so crowded. You'll probably be tempted to stay put for a while, relaxing in one of the Mediterranean's quietest corners.

Ibiza Town

The island's capital and main centre, Ibiza Town (Eivissa), is neatly divided into two areas. There is the old town—the Dalt Vila—and La Marina, the harbour. Most visitors guiding themselves through a sightseeing day in Ibiza Town arrive by bus from one of the outlying resorts. The buses stop either at the station on Isidoro Macabich, or—in the case of the small blue buses—opposite the *Delegación del Gobierno* building on the same avenue.

Isidoro Macabich intersects avinguda Ignacio Wallis; turn down it to the right and a few hundred metres later you'll come to passeig Vara del Rey, a favourite spot to while time away in the town.

As you'll see, this modest boulevard is where the local youngsters get together to decide how to spend the evening. On one side a news agent offers a wide selection of European publications, while in the middle of this pleasant promenade stands an old-fashioned,

Panoramic view of port and harbour (below); down at the quay there's other scenery to enjoy (right).

ISLAND HIGHLIGHTS

Ibiza

Ibiza Town. The harbour, La Marina, and the atmospheric, old-world streets of Sa Penya. When it all gets too much, relax at a waterside café. (See pages 26-36)

Dalt Vila. The old, walled town, now part of Ibiza Town, with its sturdy defences, cathedral, and museums. (See page 31)

Sant Antoni Abad. Fishing village turned resort, a yacht-filled bay, fishing and ferry boats, and good beaches. (See page 36)

Coniera. Sant Antoni's now-uninhabited island, where General Hannibal is said to have been born. Good for escaping the crowds and for walks among wild flowers and lizards. (See page 39)

Santa Eulària del Riu. A former market centre and the island's first town to attract foreign visitors, now boasting a fine selection of restaurants. (See page 40)

Sa Talaia. Also known as Atalaya, at 475 metres (1,560 feet) the highest point on the island, a challenging drive and/or hike, and offering magnificent views. (See page 44)

Es Cuieram. A secluded cave—used as a burial ground by the Carthaginians. Treasures uncovered here are now on view in the archaeological museum in Dalt Vila. (See page 48)

Las Salinas. Large salt flats found on both Ibiza and Formentera. (See pages 52 and 66)

Formentera

Far de la Mola. A 19th-century lighthouse which was featured in Jules Verne's *Journey Round the Solar System*; occupying a splendid position with wonderful views of Formentera. (See page 63)

Ca Na Costa. Prehistoric stone circle dating from c.2000 B.C. and currently being excavated, but open for viewing. (See page 66)

rousing **monument** to one of the island's few native sons who was successful in making a mark on Spanish history. The local hero, called Joaquín Vara de Rey, was a Spanish general who died defending the colony of Cuba against the Americans in the war of 1898.

On one side of the street are several outdoor cafés where a *café con leche* can be stretched over a whole morning of basking in the sun, postcard writing, map reading, or watching the crowds. The cafés situated nearest to the port attract the chic and sophisticated,

Even in death Joaquín Vara de Rey urges troops on. Dalt Vila's cathedral (opposite, in box).

among others, who sit at tables covered with yellow tablecloths and are served by waiters who, with exaggerated formality by local standards, are smartly decked out in bow ties and white jackets. Here, also, the town tycoons transact business in the civilized Spanish way: over Sherry or brandy.

After a coffee break and an eyeful of the passing crowds, it's time to begin an unpackaged tour of the town. The most logical place to start is down at the **harbour**. The port is virtually round the corner from the *passeig*.

An imposing pier in the centre of the dock area serves the liners from Palma, Barcelona, Valencia, and other scheduled ferry points. The passenger terminal is a modern building

On la calle Mayor in La Marina, look beyond the souvenir shops for more memorable sights.

with a restaurant on top. At any time at least one of the white ships is loading or unloading cars, cargo, or passengers, so there's always plenty of maritime action for you to savour at leisure.

In front of the terminal and now serving as a traffic roundabout is the **Corsair Obelisk** (*Obelisco a los Corsarios*)—believed to be the world's only monument in praise of privateers (see page 21).

Inland from here is the heart of the district called **La Marina**, which genuinely looks the part of a Mediterranean port. If you look beyond the souvenir shops for the moment, there are traditional sights to remember here: women in black who blend into the shadows, fishermen coming home from the sea, and everywhere the typical white houses bedecked with flower pots on wrought-iron balconies.

Don't forget to explore the hilly, narrow streets of the arm of land called **Sa Penya** occupied by many Ibizan fishermen and their families. Be warned, though—the laundry drip-drying from upper floors may splash you; children, dogs, and cats may get in your way; and the aromas of coffee, spices, fish, and baking bread may distract you. If the senses, to say nothing of the feet, need a break, relax on the waterfront with its abundance of open-air cafés. At night this district is a popular entertainment area. A few streets back into the town from the passenger terminal and the Corsair Obelisk is the inevitable, quaint Old Market. This is the old farmer's market (*mercado payes*) where friendly fruit, vegetable, and flower sellers set up their stands. The early morning is its busiest and most colourful time—an adventure in itself.

Dalt Vila

Located opposite the market is the principal entrance to the walled city, **Dalt Vila**, the old town of Ibiza. A ceremonial ramp leads across what used to be a moat into an impressive gateway, over the **Portal de las Tables**, the arch with a Latin inscription dating the wall to 1585, during the reign of King

Down at the harbour there are plenty of maritime sights to occupy your eyes.

*There's no knowing what delights you may find
around the corner in Ibiza's old town.*

Philip II of Spain. Standing on either side are headless, grace-
fully robed, white marble statues. They were unearthed on the
spot during a 16th-century construction project. According to
the barely decipherable Latin inscriptions, one of the statues
honours a Roman senator; the other is a tribute from an aris-
tocratic Roman family to Juno, the Roman goddess.

Ibiza's **seven-bulwark defences** are almost completely intact. There are three ancient gates into the city, and historians claim the Carthaginians initially constructed a wall here, though there are no remains of it. The Moors built a second wall, of which towers and remnants are still evident today. The present bulwarks date back to the year 1554, when Charles V, Holy Roman emperor, ordered that the 3½-metre-thick (6-foot) wall be reconstructed. The fortifications are a prime surviving testimony to the military technology of the time and have been proclaimed a national monument.

The tunnel through the great wall leads to a classic quadrangle fit for royal reviews. These days there's no more pomp under the porticos; instead, a variety of artisans vie for display space to peddle their jewellery and leatherwork, which is often relatively original and cheap. The **Patio de Armas**, or arsenal square, as the quad is called, leads into the first of a number of wide, open plazas which come upon you unannounced as you climb the maze of narrow alleys.

In the old town of steep, cobbled streets, curious dead ends, and unexpected vistas, a map isn't really necessary. The most important directions are simply up and down: up leads eventually to the cathedral and fortress commanding the hilltop, and down inevitably leads to one of three gates through the wall to the new town. The variations are almost infinite, and this is one time when wrong turns can actually be recommended, for every zig-zag is likely to bring another delight—a sweep of bougainvillaea, a Baroque doorway, a fashionable restaurant, or a new perspective on the sea and city below.

When you reach an impressive plaza with a 16th-century church and whitewashed town hall, you may feel that you've come to the top of the town—but you haven't. Catch your

> **When visiting churches, shorts, backless dresses and tank tops should not be worn.**

An Ibiza man takes a break in front of his home in the Old City.

breath here and admire the view down the cliffside from the edge of the city wall before continuing to ascend the narrow streets.

Suddenly you'll find yourself in another cobbled square. The **cathedral** on your right was built in the 13th century on the site of a Roman temple and Moorish mosque. It was subsequently renovated in the 16th and 18th centuries. The resulting architectural eccentricities on the outside are matched in interest by a number of medieval works of art inside (admission fee). More works can be seen in the museum attached to the cathedral (admission is around 100 pesetas). One oddity to note: the church is called *la catedral de Santa Maria de las Neus* (Our Lady of the Snows)—a rather offbeat choice of a patron saint for this sunny part of the world.

Across the square is a **museum** (*Museo Arqueològic de Dalt Vila*), which houses one of Ibiza's two archaeological collections (together constituting one of the world's great treasuries of Carthaginian art; see also page 37). All the relics on display were discovered on the island; they range from statues and urns to priceless jewellery and coins.

Many of the items are self-explanatory, which is fortunate as most descriptions are printed in Spanish only. Keep in mind the formula for dates: *III siglo a. J.C.* means third century B.C.; *XII siglo d. J.C.* means 12th century A.D.

The museum is compact enough to be covered in half an hour. Later on, try to pick your way over to Portal Nou, another gateway through the great wall, where you'll find yourself in the modern part of town in the middle of offices, luxury apartments, and shops. Four (long) streets away is the **Museo Monografic Puig des Molins**, a modern, spacious "new town" museum built on the edge of a particularly attractive hill, covered with olive trees wild flowers and which is known as **Puig des Molins** (Hill of the Windmills). Here the Carthaginians, and later the Romans, buried their dead with respectful ritual (see also pages 14-15). The artefacts displayed in the museum were all unearthed on the spot, and again, the inscriptions are in Spanish only.

The Portal Nou of Ibra Castle on Ibiza is prominent among the island's remaining fortifications.

Outside and around the corner of the building you'll find a cavelike entrance to the necropolis itself, where several typical burial chambers have been cleared and illuminated; in all there are some 4,000 vaults. After you've seen the works of art which were buried next to the bodies, the crypt shouldn't seem too gloomy a sight.

If you feel a little claustrophobic though, then wander to the far side of the hill for a view of the sea. Nearby is the beach of Figueretes (translated as "the little fig trees"), a popular place for bathing.

Sant Antoni Abad

Until the 1960s, Sant Antoni was a fishing village tucked into the pine trees at one end of a magnificent bay. Nowadays the bay is so cluttered with all kinds of yachts, fishing boats, sailing boats, ferry boats, glass-bottom boats, and even workaday freighters that the town has become something of a full-fledged Mediterranean resort of white skyscrapers. Rather than being a capital or trade centre, though, Sant Antoni is the throbbing heart of package-tour Ibiza, and instead of occupying just a corner of the bay, the town extends for miles.

The newer hotels have been built on distant beaches, providing doorstep swimming and sunbathing but requiring a ride to the shopping and nightlife. Conversely, if you're staying in town, you'll have to travel to find a desirable beach. Bus services go everywhere, and there are ferry connections, too. Either way, because of the distances involved it's worthwhile taking time to plan each day's programme.

The town itself is a hotch potch of old stucco houses and luxurious new buildings. Traditionally, activity was centred four streets up the hill from the seafront. The **14th-**

A snowflake-shaped window of la cathedral de Santa Maria de las Neus (Our Lady of the Snows).

MUSEUMS AND GALLERIES

Museo Arqueològic de Dalt Vila, at the top of the walled old town of Ibiza. Exhibits from locations all over the island, especially terra cottas and fertility figures from outlying sanctuaries and necropolises, plus a selection of Roman and Arabic artefacts. Open 10am-1pm.

Museo Monografic Puig des Molins, Via Romana. Articles discovered in the Carthaginian necropolis nearby: scarabs, unguent jars, jewellery, mirrors, and razors—even highly ornate sarcophagus handles. The richest trove of all is the superb collection of terra cottas. Be sure to take a look at the powerfully modelled series of goddesses, imperial in their elaborate necklaces, gold nose rings, and earrings. Open winter 4pm-7pm and in summer 5pm-8pm. While you're on the spot, you may want to visit the necropolis proper, where several burial chambers are open to view. The largest of them, up to 4½ metres deep, held several sarcophagi and a whole array of funerary furniture.

Museo Catedral, adjacent to Ibiza's cathedral at the summit of the old town; obligatory "donation" at the door. Contains municipal and church memorabilia. The star item in the collection is a monstrance (receptacle for the host) from Majorca. This prized example of medieval silverware probably dates back to the late 15th century. Open daily in summer 10am-1pm, and in winter Tuesday and Friday only 10am-1pm.

Museo Arte Contemporaneo, *Sala de Armas* (arsenal) alongside the city wall, just inside the old town. Modern art, one-man shows, and group exhibitions in a venerable setting. Open 10am-2pm and 5pm-7pm; Saturday 10am-1:30pm.

Art galleries. These are found in Ibiza Town and on the road to Sant Josép and Sant Miquel, as well as in Sant Antoni and Santa Eulària. Special shows are advertised. The island attracts artists of all styles and levels of expertise, and the sheer volume of their output is prodigious. Ibiza's artists also display their works in many tourist hotels and expatriate bars.

A diving boat sits idle at its mooring off the coast of Sant Antoni Abad.

century church, white and solid, is fronted by an attractive patio accentuating its gentle arches. Like many of Ibiza's churches, it was built as a combination house of worship and fortress.

The waterfront provides a pleasant sightseeing stroll. At the imposing, modern jetty you can gaze on a dreamworthy fleet of sailing boats and motor yachts. Some are designed for the daring, others for the cocktails-on-the-poop-deck crowd. Either way, it's cheap entertainment—there's no charge for boat watching.

The centre of activity is the **maritime promenade** (*passeig Marítim*), a bayfront park area reclaimed from the sea and now covered with trees, flowers, a fountain, benches, and a proliferation of outdoor cafés and restaurants.

This is where the small ferry boats—mostly converted fishing boats—compete for passengers. They operate to beaches near and far (usually, but not necessarily, the farther the better), and you'll find that there's a beach for every taste. Families with children might look for the gentlest incline of sand and the tiniest ripple of wavelets, while the snorkellers will probably be happier with a rocky coastline that attracts interesting sealife. All the beaches served by public transport have snack bars, beach chairs for hire, and umbrellas and additional amenities to one degree or another.

Note that *no* Ibiza beach maintains lifeguards.

The municipal bus station is next to the bayfront promenade, virtually on the sea itself. Buses to the beaches are cheaper and faster than the ferries, if less adventurous. However, service is

Have a sit-down, go for a dive—Ibiza has all the ingredients for a sunny seaside holiday.

restricted to beaches close to Sant Antoni. Due to geographical and historical factors, no one has ever built a round-the-coast road, thus many of the best beaches can be reached only by dusty trails more suitable for horses and carts than buses.

> **Signs:**
> *Ilegada* - **arrival**
> *Salida* - **departure**

Dominating the mouth of Sant Antoni Bay is the gaunt silhouette of the island of **Coniera**, or Conejera (meaning "rabbit's warren" or "burrow"). According to legend this uninhabited island was the birthplace of the great Carthaginian warrior Hannibal. Its other claim to fame is an automatic lighthouse whose signal can be seen 48 km (30 miles) away.

From Sant Antoni, Coniera appears to be almost hopelessly inhospitable, but a tiny hidden harbour makes it possible for boats to moor here. The island is well covered with tenacious pines, a delightful variety of wild flowers, and crowds of friendly lizards. The swimming is unsuitable for children, and the area has an overpopulation of sea urchins whose spiny quills are a menace to tender feet.

Santa Eulària del Riu

Tourists arriving in Santa Eulària may be forgiven if they wander about looking for the centre of town. It's not at the top of the hill, where a medieval fortress-church makes a pretty picture against the blue sky, and it's not at the seafront, where a flower-decked promenade overlooks a thin crescent of sandy beach.

If the island's second largest town has any centre at all, it's the sleepy square in front of the sagging old police barracks. The monument in the tiny plaza recalls a shipwreck of 1913, and a fountain on the far side features bizarre fish statues complete with jets of water which spurt from their mouths. Across the main road is the start of a boulevard laid out in the style of Barcelona's gracious *Ramblas*, but in tiny Santa Eulària the effect is somewhat muted. The tree-lined avenue extends less than three blocks to the sea.

Santa Eulària was the first village in Ibiza to attract foreign visitors—decades before the invention of the package tour—and a significant (and in some cases notorious) colony of foreign artists and writers has grown up here, scattered around the local area. One fortunate result of this community's influence has been the proliferation of good restaurants and interesting bars from which to choose.

In the past, Santa Eulària was primarily a market centre for the rich farms of the northeastern quadrant of the island. Now it has become the shopping centre for tourists based as

Among the various arts and crafts to be found on the island earthenware figures prominently.

far up and down the coast as the resort areas of Es Canar (or Es Caná) and Cala Llonga, both of which are linked to Santa Eulària by bus and ferry.

The only "must" in the village is the old **white church** on the hilltop, which is surrounded by those distinctive cube-shaped houses that are so typical of Ibicenco architecture. The ensemble looks different from each direction and at various times of day, and has inspired a hundred different artists and every amateur photographer within range. Some of the old houses on the hilltop

Visions of Ibiza in San Eulària del Riu—cube-shaped houses in the sun, and the peaceful harbour at dusk.

are admirably decorated with flower gardens, and all have a panoramic view of the sea or mountains, or both.

From the top of Puig de Missa you can look down onto Santa Eulària's noted "river" (a trickle, in fact) and the two bridges that span it. The modern bridge, just wide enough for two cars to pass, parallels a low footbridge which is apparently of Roman construction. According to island legend the low bridge was built in one furious night by the devil himself. If you're not one to be put off by superstition, stroll down to the old cobbled bridge and cross over into a quieter, more peaceful world.

Inland

Two roads connect Ibiza Town with Sant Antoni, the shorter route passing through

> **Fuel types for cars/trucks:**
> unleaded (*sin plomo*),
> regular (*gasolina*),
> premium (*super*).
> diesel (*gas-oil*)

Sant Rafel, a village whose white church is relatively modern, but stately in a Spanish colonial way. A sightseeing bonus here is that from the plaza in front of the church there's an unexpectedly stirring aerial view of Ibiza Town. Orange groves sprawl on both sides of the Ibiza–Sant Rafel road, cutting through the attractive, parched landscape. The drawback is that this is Ibiza's main east–west thoroughfare: traffic can be heavy and drivers somewhat capricious. Watch out for cars passing illegally and other potential dangers.

The more circuitous road between Ibiza and Sant Antoni runs in sight of **Sant Agustín**. There's not much to the village, though the site is attractive. You may want to visit the church, which is the area's most prominent structure. If you walk to the rear door and rouse the priest who lives at the back in stoical underemployment, he'll open the entrance to the sanctuary and leave you to inspect the blue-and-white tiles on the walls, the Baroque-style altar, and his own minute kitchen be-

The 15th-century church in Jésus is often closed, but visitors who find it open will see the island's only major work of art.

yond. Have a look, too, at the round defence tower across the road, which has been converted for use as a family dwelling.

Farther along, you come to **Sant Josép**, a village known for its handicrafts where several shops sell local embroidery and souvenirs. Not far from Sant Josép, just off the highway, is **Cova Santa** (Holy Cave). Unfortunately, nobody seems to know how it got its name. Whatever the story, this privately owned cave, of modest proportions, is open to tourists for a small fee.

Another side trip along the Sant Josép road leads to **Sa Talaia** (or Atalaya), highest point on the island. A chancy road winding up to the 475-metre (1,560-foot) summit is likely to test the engine and suspension of your car, as well as your own persistence. The view of Ibiza, the sea, and the Spanish mainland is worth it, however.

A short drive or a hefty hike north of Ibiza Town is the village of **Jésus**, with a particularly moody **15th-century church**. Like many of the rural churches, it's often closed and locked. If you're lucky enough to gain entry, you'll see the only major work of art on the whole island: the **Gothic triptych**, or altar retable, which is attributed to the artist Rodrigo de Osona from Valencia.

Most of the churches on Ibiza are worth a visit for their architectural, scenic, or historical merits. Note the black crosses painted on the white walls of houses that are situated near a church, reminders of the devotional stations of the cross celebrated on Good Friday.

A few miles southwest of Ibiza Town is the medieval church of **Sant Jordi**, combining gracious arches with no-nonsense defensive bulwarks. On the northern side of the island, the 14th-century **church of Sant Miquel** affords a hilltop view of the distant sea. The cruciform edifice is graced with black-and-white fresco decorations, and in the churchyard there is a fascinating collection of antiques, including a wine press and a grain mill. The church's ample patio, dating from the 18th century, is now taken over regularly for folklore exhibitions in which a group of dancers perform to the vigorous accompaniment of traditional musical instruments (see page 79).

The church of Sant Miquel offers antiques displays and folklore exhibitions.

Houses are sparse — in terms of both furniture and build — from here across the fertile valley to the sea.

Some of the homes have their own built-in baking ovens, which are still used daily. The pattern of cobblestone and brick on the floor of some barns is worth a peek.

You may want to visit some of the other inland hamlets— Santa Inés, Sant Joan, and Sant Carles, to name just three. Each has the ubiquitous historic church, a bar-restaurant, and a shop or two. Villagers are generally happy to see tourists, welcoming them with a certain friendly curiosity.

A Round Trip

If you've a boat and plenty of time to explore Ibiza's 170 km (105 miles) of coastline, so much the better. You still can reach many of its fine beaches and much of its glorious coastline. But note: in the absence of a coastal road, you often have to go far inland if you want to travel from one beach to another.

To start at the top of the compass and work clockwise around the island: the northernmost tourist centre is **Porti-natx** (pronounced port-ee-NATCH). To get there from the

---

Wildlife Watch

Ibiza claims a unique zoological attraction, the celebrated Ibicenco hound. Skinny as a greyhound, long-snouted, with alert big ears and eyes as mysterious as a Siamese cat's, this hungry-looking dog can trace its history back thousands of years. Yet, it's said to be less intelligent than most common mongrels.

There are no dangerous animals, poisonous insects or plants on Ibiza, and the only reptiles are harmless lizards, of which there are two dozen varieties, usually found sunning themselves on rocks or foraging among pine cones. One species of lizard may be found in your hotel, possibly clinging to the ceiling. Remember: DO NOT DISTURB—these fellows are useful allies— they catch mosquitoes.

Birdwatchers will enjoy classifying a variety of species that use the Balearics as a stopover during migration.

The beautiful cove of Cala de Sant Vicenç features good,
sandy beaches surrounded by rocky, green hills.

fertile farmland of the centre of the island you drive over substantial hills, alongside cliffs, and finally down to an unexpectedly placid sea. The natural beauty of the area—sandy beaches, weird rock formations, and plenty of juniper and pine trees—hasn't escaped the developers' notice, but the local guides still won't allow you to miss this site's two historical claims to fame. In 1929, during Spanish naval manoeuvres just off Ibiza, King Alfonso XIII came ashore here. Immediately, the name of the place was officially changed to Portinatx del Rey (of the king). Slightly more recently, part of the film *South Pacific* was shot on the beach at Portinatx.

The next major point of interest is **Cala de Sant Vicenç**, a splendid cove which is now a resort centre. While excep-

Escaping from it all: a dwelling nestling atop Serra de la Mala Costa

tionally hilly and circuitous, the road is good enough to handle a stream of tourist buses, and the beach itself is likely to be crowded. Up in the hills behind Cala Sant Vicenç — a rough hike over difficult terrain — is a cave called **Es Cuieram** (see also pages 14-15). A great many archaeological treasures have been unearthed here on the grounds of an ancient temple dedicated to the Carthaginian goddess Tanit, and most of the artefacts can be viewed at the archaeological museum in Dalt Vila. Meanwhile, the cave itself is a good place to seek temporary shelter from the midday sun.

Much of the coastline south from Cala Sant Vicenç is good, sandy beach. Areas served by roads have been built up and tend to be crowded at the height of summer. You have to wander farther afield to find peace and quiet, to say nothing of seclusion on the sand and a place for your beach towel.

Just about directly offshore from here lies the island of **Tagomago**, now linked to the "mainland" of Ibiza by regular excursion boats. Although the beach at Tagomago is too narrow for sunbathing, the swimming is superb. It's worth the trouble to ramble up to the extraordinary lighthouse at the top of the hill past various abandoned farms, wild flowers, and sweeping sea vistas.

Es Canar, the official Ibicenco spelling for a variously misspelt beach, has become a major tourist centre, with abundant nightlife, that now sprawls along several beaches. There's a popular weekly market in nearby **Punta Arabí**, to which special bus services and excursions run from Santa Eulària. Beware of gold watches and watch your belongings carefully—pickpockets prowl here.

Hikers may want to try the coastal path from Es Canar all the way to Santa Eulària and beyond. It winds its way past piney coves, mysterious cliffs, and quiet beaches. For some

---

From Witches to Whitewash

Superstitious country folk on Ibiza carry on elements of pagan witchcraft. In many Ibicenco hamlets, old women credited with supernatural powers treat ailing people and animals. These witch doctors use incantations and herbal medicines.

Another tradition says certain bottles contain *diablillos*, little devils or imps. If a housewife opens the bottle without following the proper procedure she is plagued by all manner of minor domestic problems.

Every springtime, the hardy women of Ibiza set out with almost religious enthusiasm to whitewash their houses. There's a suspicion among some anthropologists that the whitewash craze may derive from some remote Punic ritual. Local poet Fajarnes Cardona termed it, "That whiteness, an exorcism of all that's sordid."

Architects from abroad point out that each house represents a conjunction of one-room units, infinitely expandable to suit conditions. Instead of the traditional patio, Ibiza has opted for open verandahs with stately arches. Triangular-topped chimneys, outside staircases, and cubist tendencies have inspired modern architects near and far.

From hotel to beach and from beach to water— Ibiza's various hotels have their guests in mind.

this may sound like hard work, but don't despair: beach-bar refreshment is never far away.

Cala Llonga, to the south of Santa Eulària, is just what its name describes —a long cove which, from several vantage points, looks like a Norwegian fjord. Hotels and apartment construction push back into the hills, and locals as well as day-trippers from Santa Eulària throng the deep, sandy beach. But thankfully, Cala Llonga's worst problems are a thing of the past, and pollution, which was once rampant, has been halted by the construction of a sewage plant some distance away.

An impressive rocky coastline with a backdrop of verdant hills continues southward to **Talamanca**, a heavily developed beach with a fine view of Ibiza Town. On the other side of the capital is the hotel complex of **Figueretas**, and then the long, straight seafront beach of **Playa D'En Bossa**. This was once the scene of a famous misdevelopment plan, when a 600-room luxury hotel had to be demolished just as it was ready to open for business, since it had mistakenly been built directly on the flight path to Ibiza airport.

ISLAND BEACHES

Ibiza

Cala Bassa. Long, gently sloping beach, suited for children.

Cala Conta. Sandy beach, suitable for children.

Cala Llonga. A shallow bay, good for young children. Amenities include restaurants and sunbeds.

Cala Tárida. Activity-oriented beach, plenty of watersports, popular with the active crowd.

Cala Badella. Popular but often busy beach offering lots of amenities: bars, *pedalos*, windsurfing.

Es Canar. Popular beach and cove with fine sands and a backdrop of pinewoods.

Playa Cavallet. The island's official nudist beach, complete with amenities, but offering little shade.

Playa D'En Bossa. Known as the island's longest beach (2½ km/1½ miles), close to Ibiza Town and very busy. Popular especially for its lively beach bar.

Playa las Salinas. Located past the saltflats in the south of the island. Good sands, lots of amenities, especially popular with the locals.

Formentera

Cala Sahona. Attractive, sandy beach, the most popular on Formentera and often busy.

Platja de Mitjorn. A pebbly beach, Formentera's longest (8 km/5 miles), stretched around a wide bay.

Playa Es Pujols. Arguably the best beach on the island: good sands, shallow water, and lots of amenities.

Overlooking the inlet at Port de Sant Miquel,
where clear waters lap the rocky shores.

ming pools and bar service—which is just as well, since the
beach couldn't comfortably accommodate them all at once.

Other than walking in the wooded hills, the most popular
local attraction is the **Cova de Can Marça**, a cave where
sound and light effects enhance the natural wonders of sta-
lagmites and stalactites.

FORMENTERA

Less than four nautical miles separate Formentera, with its long sandy beaches, from Ibiza. The people and the language are the same, yet the two islands couldn't be farther removed. Formentera has no airport—nor are there any plans to build one—and a ferry and hydrofoil service provide the only inter-island links. This Balearic outpost boasts a sizeable salt lake but no fresh water. Cisterns, some of them dating from Moorish times, catch whatever rain falls from the sky, and when needed, supplementary water supplies are shipped in to this desert island.

> **Full tank, please!**
> *Llénelo, por favor.*
> (**lyay**nayloa por fahb**hor**)

Potential water shortages have not been enough to stop the developers, however, and hotel complexes and scores of new apartment blocks line the beaches of Es Pujols, Mitjorn, Es Caló, and Cala Sahona. These centres attract most of the tourists and summer residents, who swell the permanent population of roughly 5,000 to 20,000 or more. The impact of this seasonal influx of tourists (mainly German, British, and French) has been dramatic. Still, there's room to spare on Formentera.

Constrained by the limited water supply and the ab-

The deep blue sea provides a striking contrast to the barren cliffs of Formentera.

sence of an airport, the pace of construction and change have been kept within reasonable bounds, with regulations stipulating, for instance, that buildings may not rise higher than four storeys. Traffic, also, has been controlled, and if you're staying here you might want to consider getting around by bicycle; there's no better way to explore an island that measures no more than 20 km (12½ miles) from end to end, one-fifth

Isolated woods such as these in Formentera offer peace and quiet away from the beaches.

the size of Ibiza. Alternatively, choose from small Land Rover–type vehicles, scooters, and mopeds. If you come to Formentera just for a day, then the best option is car rental (or scooter/moped): although the island is small, it is too large to see all in one day by bicycle. Don't rely on public transport, either, because the bus service is extremely limited.

But most visitors prefer to linger in Formentera. They're attracted by the sun and sea, by the incomparable beaches, and by some of the finest windsurfing and scuba diving in the Mediterranean. Beautiful

Resolutely holding on to their old Mediterranean ways, the people of Formentera still fish regularly.

sandy beaches like Platja de Mitjorn go on for miles. Here and elsewhere, you'll see many nude sunbathers, and toplessness is the order of the day. So far, nude bathing has been legalized only on the isolated beaches of Illetas and Llevant, but it is practised virtually everywhere. As a rule, officials take no notice and you're free to sunbathe as you please.

For all Formentera's happy-go-lucky ways, traditions are still firmly entrenched. Farmers continue as precariously as ever, scratching a living from the arid, rocky soil. Wheat, barley, and oats are the most significant crops, wheat having been cultivated since Roman times, when the island was

ISLAND FLORA

The rewards of a close-up look at the countryside of Ibiza include a botanical treasury. If you're interested in plants and flowers and want to know what's in bloom when—here's a calendar:

January: mimosa bushes covered with yellow puffballs.

February: white and pink almond blossoms — unforgettable as a blizzard; and on the hills giant blue iris, yellow gorse, and tiny bee orchids create an Impressionist landscape.

March–April: fields of daisies—even daisy bushes—and pink field gladioli announce spring on Ibiza.

May–June: the striking scarlet of flowering pomegranate trees contrasts with the red of poppies in the corn fields and the bright yellow flowers of the prickly pear.

July–August: now the garden flowers bloom: honeysuckle in yellow and cream; the blue, trumpet-shaped morning glory, and pink and white oleander; bougainvillaea starts to sprout bright green leaves and scarlet flowers; even when you're on the beach there are signs of spring from the white, sweet-scented sea daffodil pushing up out of the sand.

September: rainbows of petunias, geraniums, and dahlias; and look out for the white spikes of the yucca plant.

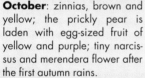

October: zinnias, brown and yellow; the prickly pear is laden with egg-sized fruit of yellow and purple; tiny narcissus and merendera flower after the first autumn rains.

November: in shady woods, white and pink heather hugs the ground; rosemary bushes, covered with tiny blue flowers, dot open areas.

December: orange and lemon trees bear fruit.

Almost year-round in the most unexpected places—in tiny crevices between rocks, alongside every road and path—the wildflowers, sometimes almost microscopic, offer a wild bouquet of colour and life.

The superb array of blooms to be found on Ibiza. Clockwise from bottom left: morning glory ; typical Ibicenco view; prickly pear with its curious yellow and purple fruit: the delicacy of a pink rose; and yellow mimosa.

59

known as *Frumenteria,* or "wheat producer." Other crops include grapes used for Formentera's distinctive dry red wine, *vino de pagés*, and almond and fig trees thrive, but the olive trees here bear little fruit.

Life still revolves around stuccoed farmhouses with tiled roofs and columned verandahs. Lush red, juicy tomatoes, threaded together in garlands, hang from the rafters to dry, while almonds are shelled for sale to tourists, together with honey, figs, and the fruit of an industrious winter's knitting: gloves, scarves, caps, socks, and pullovers fashioned from local, coarse, cream-coloured homespun wool. No matter

Houses like this one are typical among Formentera's farmers, who have cultivated wheat since Roman times.

how enthusiastically they welcome tourism, the islanders seem reluctant to abandon a rural lifestyle— which further enhances the charm of the islands.

Island Sights

From Ibiza Town, ferries and hydrofoils depart frequently for the port of **La Sabina**, a journey of around one hour or 25 minutes, respectively. The route passes in sight of two uninhabited

The church at Sant Francesc Xavier has an extraordinary presence.

islands: Es Vedrà, which hovers like an apparition on the horizon off to the west, and **Espalmador**, which is popular with yachtsmen for its white-sand beach. Passengers disembark onto the quayside at La Sabina, taking in at a glance the languorous activity of the harbour and the spate of construction that is changing the skyline of the town. Here you can rent a car, scooter, moped, or bicycle, or catch the bus. The port serves as the only terminal for Formentera's limited public transport system (which is not reliable). There are also cars, scooters, and taxis available for hire.

Follow the main road inland past the island's lone petrol (gasoline) station (which is closed after dark!) to the town of **Sant Francesc Xavier,** or San Francisco Javier. The population of Formentera's chief city has expanded to around 1,000, and there is a new town hall. Parked at the back is the jaunty Land Rover that serves as a fire engine— the first on Formentera and just one of the beneficial side effects of the tourist boom.

The most prominent structure built in Sant Francesc is its **18th-century church**. This fortress of whitewashed stone, squat as a bunker, sheltered townsfolk at times when pirate raids threatened. Now tourists descend on the town's three main streets, and a growing number of souvenir shops proclaims the new order of things.

From Sant Francesc, take the road that leads southwest to Cap Berbería (the southernmost point in the Balearics). Just over 1½ km (1 mile) out of town you pass the turn to the small sandy bay of **Cala Sahona**, which is framed by cliffs of red rock and hotel and holiday apartment blocks. Except for Cala Sahona, this part of the island is sparsely

The Sant Francesco Xavier church—rich in history as well as art—is the most prominent building in town.

populated. There are a few farms, scattered fields marked by stone walls, and corrals enclosing sheep, goats, and pigs. The parched landscape grows ever more desolate as you approach **Cap Berbería**, and the road deteriorates until it's no more than a dusty track. The cape itself is the haunt of wild goats and the site of an isolated lighthouse and a watchtower, built high above the sea.

After the solitary beauty of Cap Berbería comes **Platja de Mitjorn**, a sublime arc of sand 8 km (5 miles) long, popular with vacationers in summer. The area has been developed with a number of hotels, notably Club Hotel La Mola, Formentera's most luxurious resort, Hotel Formentera Playa, and the Mar-y-land complex. Continue east to the village of **Nostra Senyora del Pilar** and on to **Far de la Mola**, an old lighthouse built in 1861, still in operation. A veteran keeper lives on the premises, tending the beacon that is visible 65 km (40 miles) out to sea. Far de la Mola figures in the Jules Verne adventure *Journey Round the Solar System*, a fact commemorated by a monument nearby. Time and technological advances have passed the lighthouse by, and it's not difficult to see why it caught Verne's imagination. Literary connections apart, the site has a certain splendour, affording as it does ravishing views over Formentera and out across the sea.

Platja de Mitjorn stretches some 8 km (5 miles) and includes a number of hotels and luxury resorts.

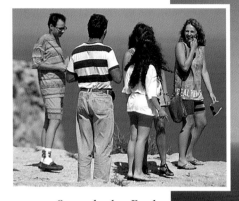

On a calm day, Far de la Mola affords beautiful views of the pristine blue Mediterranean.

More glorious still is the panorama from the **mirador** above **Es Caló**. This lookout is one of the highest spots on the island. You can't miss the lookout point: it stands right alongside the road in full view of the narrow spine of land that connects eastern Formentera to the island's western half. The white expanse of Platja de Mitjorn, clearly visible on the southern side, is paralleled by the rocky strip of beach on the Es Caló side. Es Caló's tiny harbour dates from Roman times, when it was Formentera's only port. Nowadays it is yet another target for tourist development, and there are already several

small hotels and apartment complexes set amongst the pinewoods.

After Es Caló, return along the main trans-island road to **Sant Ferran**, a pleasant village with a pretty church. From there, take the road that heads back to the coast and **Es Pujols**, Formentera's premier resort village. Scores of bars, restaurants, and kiosks cater for the primarily German

*A breathtaking view
from the mirador above
Es Caló.*

tourists, and the beach is usually awash with lounge chairs and sunbaked bodies, *pedalos*, and windsurfing gear. Farther west there are some less populous stretches where you can swim in relative seclusion or eat at a simple beach restaurant. Don't expect much in the way of facilities; these simple establishments are intended to be dismantled at the end of every season, when the area returns to its unadulterated form.

The oldest construction on Formentera—a dolmen, or prehistoric stone circle—lies not far from Es Pujols at **Ca Na Costa** (between the La Sabina road and Formentera's salt lake). Although the site is still under excavation, you can visit it. A shelter has been erected to protect the limestone monoliths from the elements. Also in the area are Formentera's salt pans, **Las Salinas**. To reach the salt lakes, follow the road on the outskirts of La Sabina before turning right, eastwards, down a rough lane, at the end of which turn left. In use since Roman times, today the salt pans are the source of 18,000 metric tons (20,000 tons) of salt a year. The salt has large crystals (which have a higher density than those from Ibiza) and is considered excellent for curing fish. The export point is, of course, La Sabina, first and last port of call on any round-island jaunt.

WHAT TO DO

SPORTS AND OUTDOOR ACTIVITIES

With sunshine throughout the year and with the temperate waters of the Mediterranean lapping its shores, Ibiza is ideal for aquatic-sports enthusiasts. Although the stress is on swimming and sailing, you may well prefer to do nothing more strenuous than lie in the sun and be a spectator.

Formentera, for its part, boasts fewer people and some of the most enticing sandy beaches, to say nothing of windsurfing and scuba diving that can't be bettered in the Balearics.

One important note of caution: the summer sun easily wreaks havoc with the unwary, and it really is a case of "only mad dogs and Englishmen," as Noel Coward put it. Leave it to the mad dogs. Half an hour in the morning and late afternoon creates the groundwork for a good tan. At all times it's

Windsurfing is a main attraction on Ibiza and Formentera.

a good idea to wear a T-shirt or something light to protect your shoulders, as well as a hat. Don't be complacent even in winter: delicate northern noses have been seen to peel under the November or March sun.

Watersports

Boating and sailing. Very few vacationers arrive in their own boats or are otherwise totally self-sufficient for sailing in the Mediterranean, but the yacht clubs and many of the beaches supply sailing boats for hire, and some also have schools. The rates are about the same as in mainland Spanish resorts, and sometimes cheaper.

According to Spanish law, only captains who have an official licence can operate motorboats. This law is rigidly enforced; consequently, motorboats are seldom available for hire to tourists.

Sailboats. Suitable for a crew of two, these are just the ticket if you want to learn to sail. Beach bars and most watersports schools rent out sailboats. Instruction is optional, but advisable for real novices.

Pedalos. These two-seat contraptions ply the seas powered by a foot-driven waterwheel. They are sufficiently stable for a young child to be aboard accompanied by an adult, and are perfect as a personalized ferry boat to reach coves for snorkelling or just to avoid the crowds. Pedalos can be hired by the hour, but you should always allow yourself plenty of time to return to shore before your rental period has expired.

Windsurfing is a major attraction on Ibiza and Formentera; equipment can be hired at *escuelas de windsurfing* as well as many resorts. This sport has more or less taken the place of waterskiing, which is not nearly as common now.

Fishing along the rocks of the coastline is a popular pursuit, no matter how unlikely the prospect of a large catch. Offshore, the

Explore the depths of the sea in a glass-bottomed boat. This one sets forth from Sant Antoni.

professional fishing business—which was once a major source of income in Ibiza—has dwindled significantly. These days, island fishmongers are just as likely to sell frozen fish from afar as the freshly caught local article. Some dawdling fishermen work the banks of Ibiza's Riu de la Santa Eulària, especially at the point where it empties into the sea, but if you're having a go yourself don't expect too much more than a nibble.

You might have more fun—and even success—"spinning" from the back of a boat; catches of brill almost half a metre (1½ feet) long are not uncommon in winter. The equipment is easily available and cheap.

Scuba diving, snorkelling. Firstly, and most important of all, note that spearfishing with scuba equipment is forbidden. Secondly, the shores of Ibiza contain so much archaeological treasure that the government keeps a sharp eye on all divers. Before you can dive underwater you need a licence from the CRIS

(*Centro de Recuperación y Investigaciones Submarinas*—Underwater Recovery and Research Centre). So be warned, the authorities take this seriously, and violators may be prosecuted.

Scuba-diving schools operate on Ibiza and Formentera, though the locations tend to change from year to year. You must apply for a licence yourself, and a medical certificate is also required.

Fortunately, the whole family can enjoy a hint of the thrills of undersea swimming. Snorkelling equipment is relatively cheap in the shops, but test the face mask carefully before you buy it. With a little practice almost anyone can flip off to an interesting rock formation and watch the multi-coloured fish pass in review. Snorkel-fishing with spear-guns is legal, but the fish, which can often be frisky with unarmed snorkellers, now know to scatter at the sight of a harpoon.

If you don't feel squeamish about it, you can prowl the rocks in shallow waters with a face mask and spear in search of squid. These tentacled creatures may look terrible under water, but once out in the air they're revealed as small and not dangerous. In winter, thousands of squid lurk among the

---

Donkey Treks

More than 50 trained donkeys work at the burro ranch near Santa Gertrudis. An outing from here includes a 20-minute ride over a mountain, followed by a wine-tasting party. Watch out for the donkey that drinks *sangría* from a *porrón* (see page 92)—quite a feat. The combination of the scenery, the ride, and the general fun and games make this a popular excursion, which you will find is organized by many travel agencies. Alternatively, if you want to drive to Santa Gertrudis yourself, it will cost you about half as much.

Using donkeys for leisure purposes is a recent development. Burros have been used as beasts of burden since the times of the ancient Egyptians. Those big-eared, sure-footed creatures can still be found on farms all over Ibiza, gainfully employed in spite of competition from tractors and trucks.

rocks in very shallow waters along the coast, and the only equipment you need to catch them is a face mask and *gancho* (hook). The problem is learning how to tell the difference between the squid and the rocks they settle in. If you can solve that one you'll have a lot of fun and a few catches too.

Going nowhere? Pedalos are a perfect way to while away a lazy afternoon.

Swimming. Most Ibiza hotels and apartment complexes offer their own freshwater pools. On Formentera, however, this is not necessarily the rule.

Amenities inevitably come hand in hand with crowds, so on the main beaches be prepared to do battle with lots of other sun-seekers, all equally happy that restaurants, toilets, showers, and changing rooms are there. Territorial rights, in the form of a deck chair, can be assured for a nominal sum.

The concept of a professional lifeguard is unknown on Ibiza and Formentera alike; some beach bars do keep first-aid supplies. Fortunately, most of the favourite beaches are well protected from waves and undertow, and slope gradually. Normally they are safe, but on a rough day, take care.

If you're willing to wander off the beaten track you should be able to find cliff-backed coves with clear, blue water or patches of sand scarcely large enough for two families.

Other Sports

Tennis. Although there are no grass courts on the islands, a number of asphalt or composition courts are available at hotels and apartment complexes.

A stroll on the promenade affords a leisurely break from the more strenuous water-oriented activities.

Courts can be hired by the hour—you'll probably have to book ahead. A few hotels offer professional coaching; prices vary greatly according to the reputation of the teacher.

Whether you take your tennis seriously or just like to hit a ball around, be careful of the midday sun. New arrivals especially should lie low during the most blistering hours to avoid burns or exhaustion.

Hunting and shooting. It's not certain which came first, the famous Ibicenco hounds or the island's craze for weekend hunting forays.

In either case, the locals set off into the hills more for the exercise than for the kill. The occasional partridge and rabbit are about the extent of the possibilities. The season runs during autumn and winter from October to February. Clay pigeon shooting is popular, too.

Check for details on hunting permits at the local tourist office (see page 123) or drop a line to ICONA, Carrer Sabino de Arana, 22, Barcelona.

Golf and miniature golf. One unexpected sight, in a remote valley near Cala Llonga, is a civilized, meticulously tended, exquisitely green golf course. Those who feel a holiday isn't the same without a game are welcome to tee off there.

If you can't get into the golf club scene, then why not try miniature golf in Sant Antoni, Santa Eulària, or Portinatx on Ibiza, and at Club La Mola on quieter Formentera.

Archery. Those who are adept with a bow and arrow can keep their hand in on Ibiza and Formentera. Check at the tourist office for details (see page 123).

Horseback riding. The countryside of Ibiza, with its gentle green hills and grid of back roads, is perfectly suited to horseback riding. You can find stables in the following places: Portinatx, Sant Antoni, Santa Gertrudis, and near Santa Eulària. In addition, there are instructors and horses suited for children.

If you're the equestrian type, then this is a good way to see the offbeat side of Ibiza — the unspoiled interior where life is still refreshingly simple.

Horse racing. Horse races are held every Sunday afternoon at the Hippodrome Ibiza, Sant Rafel. The trotting race is a particularly exciting event to watch.

SHOPPING

Shopping Hours

Shopping hours in Ibiza last from around 9:00 A.M. to 1:00 P.M. and from 4:00 to 8:00 P.M. During summer some shops remain open for an extra half hour or more in the evening to cope with the crush. Bars and cafés are usually open from as early as 8:00 A.M. until midnight or later with no break for the siesta. Most boutiques open only during the tourist season, starting at Easter and ending in November.

Best Buys

As a rule, prices on Ibiza are higher than on the Spanish peninsula, and these days you will find few real bargains.

Shoes: ordinary shoes for both men and women can be quite cheap, but anything stylish is likely to cost as much as at home. Traditional *alpargatas*—shoes of straw and hemp and a number of other ingenious indigenous materials—are just the thing for outings to the beach, shopping, or lounging around in comfort at the hotel.

Bags: The straw bags that Ibicencos and visitors hang over their shoulders for shopping or for carrying beach equipment are useful and inexpensive. They are made in several sizes—for children and adults, for carrying odds and ends, or for buying out the supermarket. Over the years these bags have proved so handy that to keep up with demand the local supply of genuine handmade bags has been augmented with imported goods.

Jewellery: Gold and silver jewellery made on the spot or elsewhere in Spain is popular for both quality and price. You will also see "hippie-made" jewellery on sale, especially at the market in Punta Arabí. Some of the artisans here look as if they're straight out of the 1960s.

Clothing: There's nothing like the trendy resort clothing available here, styled on the island by the designers of the Ad-Lib group. They are renowned as far away as New York for their Ibiza look. In another category altogether are the hand-knitted and crocheted articles made by island women.

| Signs:
rebajas -
sale |

Pottery: Locally produced pottery may also interest you. The terra-cotta bowls have centuries of tradition behind them; the ashtrays are also attractive, if obviously less authentic. Be careful what you choose, though, since inadequately fired, unglazed pottery is risky to ship or pack.

Liquor and tobacco: These are both cheap compared to European and American prices. Prices in town are low, while those at the airport duty-free shop are lower still. Imported Cuban cigars, plentiful and cheap, are a favourite take-home present, though they're still outlawed by U.S. Customs. While foreign-brand alcohol, produced under licence in Spain, sells for just a few hundred pesetas a bottle, there are more unusual local spirits that might make apt souvenirs of Ibiza. Such drinks are spiced with the island's wild herbs, result-

Ibiza's beautiful local pottery is firmly rooted in centuries of tradition.

ing in interesting and varied flavours. *Hierbas, anís seco, anís dulce,* and *frigola* are just a few names worth keeping a look-out for.

Herbs and spices: Bought off the shelf in the local supermarkets, these cost virtually nothing. Take home a bunch of tiny packets of colourful *azafrán* (saffron) and any other dried herbs you may fancy. An overpoweringly fragrant shop located in the port area of Ibiza Town stocks just about every spice known to modern man.

Local foods: A variety of local and Spanish foodstuffs can be transported home with a minimum of fuss and bother, including almonds, olives, olive oil, sausage, cheese, and dried figs. Look for these items in the picturesque open-air market of Sa

Penya (Ibiza Town) or—for a wider selection—at the bustling, covered central market in the newer part of town (carrer d'Extremadura).

Antiques: In the past there must have been intriguing opportunities to buy up Ibicenco antiques and ship them home. Nowadays it would take more time scrounging about than the average visitor is willing to invest. Browse around the shops, however, and you may find an appealing piece of old ironwork or hand carving. At the least you will always be able to take home a rusty old door key or two suitable for haunted houses, or a kitchen iron of genuine pre-electric vintage.

Where to Shop

The area around the port in Ibiza Town offers the largest choice of shops on the island. Quite a few establishments devote themselves primarily to their local customers, rather than stocking tourist extravagances. Here, too, you'll find all the boutiques that clothe Ibiza's trendier visitors.

Shopping Tips

It's always wise to price items in more than one shop before deciding what and where to buy, as costs tend to vary.

Occasionally, you will see a notice of sales—*rebajas*—in shop windows. Although legitimate sales do take place, usually at the end of the high season to dispose of unsold stock, you'll have to be a bit cautious. What seems to be a special bargain price for just "one week only" could turn out to be a year-round con. Here, too, shopping around is the best way to know a bargain if and when you see one. Haggling is now a thing of the past and unacceptable.

> A chemist's is called *farmacia* (fahr**mah**thyah), and they don't sell books, film, newspapers, toilet articles, or cosmetics.

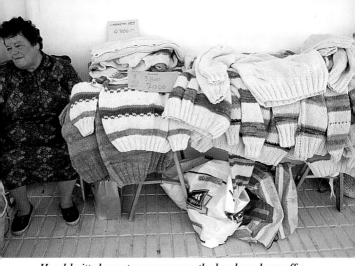

Hand-knitted sweaters are among the local goods on offer.

ENTERTAINMENT

Folklore of Ibiza

The truly local art form, found nowhere else, is Ibicenco folk singing and dancing. Regular shows take place in some villages, such as Sant Miquel and Sant Josép, and there are often special one-time performances in other towns and villages during fiestas, mostly based on saints' days and religious festivals.

First, a note about the lavish traditional costumes: the men sport red hats (similar to the Catalonian model), bandannas tied round their necks, gold-trimmed black corduroy or cotton jackets over their loose-fitting white shirts, bright red cummerbunds, baggy trousers of white linen, wide at the

Traditional costumes are an integral part of Ibicenco folk singing and dancing.

thighs but tight at the ankles, and the familiar Ibicenco straw shoes for comfort.

The costume donned by the women is more complex. It includes a long, pleated skirt of homespun wool, either black or white; an apron with complicated patterns; a fine silk, long-tasselled shawl over the shoulders; and a big lace mantilla over the head, with hair braided down the back, sometimes tied by a schoolgirl ribbon. Around the neck hang various strands of gold, a heavy golden necklace, ribbons, a gold scapular with images of saints on both sides, and a crucifix. Much of this adornment is gold filigree, like an *emprendad*, a necklace of Moorish design. In addition, the women wear various heavy rings. The costumes are so original and ornate that a fair amount of time is spent at each folklore show explaining them in detail. Even children on foot or in strollers wear a miniature version of the costumes.

The meaning of each dance is recounted, but this is usually not easy since the origins have often been forgotten. Most of the dances are suggestive of ancient courtship rituals, with the man being forceful and arrogant, the woman shyly flirta-

FESTIVALS

The following list details annual festivals held on fixed dates on Ibiza. Check with the tourist information office (see page 123) for information about other events.

May, first Sunday *Fiesta in Santa Eulària*, combining a spring festival with a flower show.

June 23, 24 *St. John the Baptist's Day*—fireworks, bonfires, and festivities in Ibiza Town and Sant Antoni. This is an important holiday for the Ibicencos, since every year on 24 June landowners and tenant farmers make their verbal contracts for the coming year.

July 16 *St. Carmen festival*—Ibiza Town, regattas held in honour of the Virgen Del Carmen. Similar celebrations are held in Sant Antoni on the following Sunday.

July 25 *Fiesta of St. James*—with procession, folk songs, and dancing on Formentera.

August 4-8 *Santa Maria de las Neus* (Our Lady of the Snows)—Ibiza Town honours its incongruously named patron saint with marching bands, fireworks, folk dances, sporting events, and religious services.

August 24 *St. Bartholomew's Day*—commemorated in Sant Antoni by various events, including a procession, high mass, concerts, fireworks, and sporting activities.

September 8 *Fiesta de Jésus*—religious and popular festival celebrated in Santa Eulària del Riu.

November 1 *All Saints Day*, Ibiza and Formentera—special cakes, pastries, and nuts sold in markets.

December 3 *Fiesta in Sant Francesc Xavier on* Formentera—with a procession, dancing, and folk songs.

tious. In one dance, the women form a circle, moving in small steps, their eyes cast down, while the men perform high kicks, sticking to the outside. Often the songs have witty, ribald lyrics likely to suffer fatally in impromptu translation.

The music is played on typically Catalonian—and in some cases uniquely Ibicencan—instruments: a wooden flute and a small drum (handled simultaneously by a single ambidextrous man), a sort of steel sabre struck in rhythm, and large castanets. The music appears to have survived fundamentally from Moorish culture, though over the centuries it has accumulated a number of extraneous elements. Some of the light-hearted songs require the singer to emit a weird, guttural "ye-ye-ye" sound.

Making your own way to the villages will cost less than if you take an organized excursion, which includes the inevitable libation of *sangría*.

Festivals

The popular *fiestas* of Ibiza are much less pretentious than the equivalent (and more famous) *ferias* of mainland Spain. With tourists in mind, several feast days now offer special

---

Nightclubs in Ibiza

Amnesia (tel. 19 80 41) *Main road Ibiza–Sant Antoni.*
Angel's *Marina de Botafoc,* contests and novelty parties.
Divino (tel. 19 01 76) *Marina de Botafoc,* exotic parties.
Es Paradis Terrenal (tel. 34 28 93) *Sant Antoni,* novelty parties, easy access from Sant Antoni hotels.
Kiss (tel. 30 64 17) *Sant Rafel,* biggest and most famous club, hosts well-known disc jockeys and live music events.
Privilege (tel. 19 80 86) *Playa D'En Bossa,* foam parties.
Space (tel. 39 67 93) *Playa D'En Bossa,* specializes in early morning parties and opens when other clubs close.

---

events and fireworks which never featured in the original celebrations. For the visitor, the most interesting observances are the modest old standbys—generally the saint's day of a village: sombre religious processions, often held by candlelight, folk music, a rash of quaint costumes. It may not be the carnival you expected, but it can be much more memorable.

Nightlife

Ibiza's many **nightclubs** attract rich and famous media celebrities, as well as virtually every other visitor to the area. Many people come to Ibiza expressly for the clubs, which run the gamut from plush to sleazy. Traditional audience participation in events such as beauty contests usually plays a part in the entertainment.

Signs:
fumadores - smoker
no fumadores - nonsmokers

Ibiza Town itself is not the place to go for the club scene, although Dalt Vila has a few gay bars and there is plenty of other entertainment available.

The undisputed centre for nightlife on the island is Sant Antoni, where establishments range from big brash nightclubs to the smaller clubs and bars with disc jockeys or live music of various kinds, including jazz.

The Playa D'En Bossa area to the west of Ibiza Town also has a lively nightlife, with Irish bars, live music, and clubs.

In the summer months a Discobus runs from Ibiza Town (from around 11:00 P.M.) to some of the major clubs, so you don't have to drive. See the box on page 80 for details of the current hot-spots.

Don't forget that many large hotels offer evening activities every night of the week, and you don't need to be a guest of the hotel to participate.

Ibiza's **casino**, handily located on the passeig Marítim, is open all year round. To gain entrance to the gaming room, you

Ibiza Town is not the best place to enjoy the night life, but its harbour is a beautiful place to visit by day.

have to present your passport or identification papers. For a small fee, you will be issued a computerized admission card, which is good for one or more days of roulette (both French and American), as well as blackjack and craps.

The stakes for many of the games are low, so you can try your hand without risking too much. Early in the evening, tourists crowd in for a look at what's going on, but as time wears on, the dyed-in-the-wool gamblers come to the fore.

Also on the premises are a nightclub with a floor show and an art gallery.

Most **films** in Ibiza's cinemas have been dubbed into Spanish. Aside from the more conventional cinemas of Ibiza Town, other places that show films on the island are old-fashioned if not picturesque. Either once or twice a week you can now see films in English in both Santa Eulària and Sant Antoni.

> **Signs:**
> *entrada* - **entrance**
> *salida* - **exit**

EATING OUT

Eating and drinking in a new part of the world can be a pleasurable adventure. It's somewhat more so on Ibiza because of the cultural mix. The cook may be from Valencia, the cuisine advertised as "French," and the customer may want nothing more daring than a steak. Thanks to Ibiza's popularity around the world, as well as its noted permanent colony of expatriates, the variety of restaurants is exceptional: French, Italian, Scandinavian, even Chinese cooking, is available. The food is usually quite good, though it can be a bit on the expensive side.

International fare is also offered in the hotels, but if you venture beyond the resort enclaves you'll be able to sample

The wines and cuisine of Ibiza are as varied as the international visitors who come to the island.

Cooking out in the open, where fish just plucked from the sea can be grilled without delay.

authentic Spanish cuisine. Make for Ibiza Town, where *tapas* bars serve a variety of typical snacks and sandwiches to a mostly local clientele, or explore the Santa Eulària area, which is renowned among Ibicencos for its eating houses. On Formentera, have a meal at a simple beach restaurant.

Eating well is a passion with the Spanish. You're not likely to go wrong if you ask local people to tell you where to find their favourite bars and restaurants.

Spanish Specialities

Gazpacho (pronounced gath-PAT-cho) is an Andalusian invention, a highly flavoured, chilled **soup** to which chopped cucumbers, peppers, tomatoes, onions, and sippets (croutons) are added to taste. It's been described as "liquid salad" and can be a rousing refresher.

Paella (pie-ALE-ya) originated in Valencia, just across the sea from Ibiza. It's named after the iron pan in which the saffron **rice** is cooked. Among the additional ingredients are morsels of squid and shrimp, mussels, rabbit, sausage, peppers, chicken, onions, peas and beans, tomatoes, garlic . . . and whatever else happens to inspire the cook at the moment.

Technically, *paella* is served only at lunchtime and always cooked to order. It takes more than half an hour, time enough to pacify your hunger with another dish for which Spain is known: *tortilla española* (Spanish omelette; no connection with Mexican tortillas). This is different from a French-style omelette, in that this one resembles a substantial egg-and-potato pie.

Since Ibiza is an island in the Mediterranean, **fish**, usually grilled and served with a salad and fried potatoes, figures most importantly—and delectably —in the local diet. Ask your waiter for the "catch of the day," and if *pez espada* (swordfish) has been hauled ashore earlier on, he'll proudly recommend a satisfying grilled steak of it. Alternatively, try *salmonete* (red mullet), *mero* (grouper), or *lenguado* (sole).

In season you can find delicious varieties of shellfish— from *langostinos* (Dublin Bay prawns) to *gambas* (prawns) and *mejillones* (mussels).

Barbecues

A popular excursion organized by tour agencies is the all-you-can-eat-and-drink barbecue outing. You will be taken to a rustic setting where meat is sizzling over glowing coals and unlimited quantities of red wine or *sangría* are waiting to be drunk. Afterwards, a band usually plays music for dancing.

You'll learn to drink wine from a *porrón* (see page 92), a glass container with a pointed spout from which the liquid arcs through the air into your open mouth—theoretically, anyway. To enjoy the experience fully, don't wear your best clothes, and remember to put a napkin around your neck.

And don't forget *calamares*, strips of squid, most commonly fried in batter (*a la romana*)—a snack or a meal in itself. By the way, if you come across a menu offering *filete de pescado a la romana con patatas fritas*, don't accuse the restaurant of putting on airs—it's the correct Spanish way to say "fish and chips."

There's plenty of **meat** on the menu as well: local pork and lamb, fowl, and game. If you prefer a beefsteak, there's a confusing list from which to choose: *chateaubriand*, *tornedos*, and *entrecôte*. The most tender cut, similar to filet mignon, is called *solomillo* (*filete*).

Ibicencan Specialities

Sofrit pagès: this hearty meat-and-potato stew is cooked with saffron, garlic, sweet pepper, cinnamon, and cloves.

Sopas: found in any restaurant is this good, cheap, local soup — of lentils, rice, butter beans, green beans — whatever may be available. If it's on the menu, try *sopa de pescado* (fish soup) or *sopa marinera* (seafood soup).

Garbanzos: a dish of chickpeas served the Ibicenco way: with parsley, oil, and garlic.

Self-Catering with Squid?

If you catch a squid (or pretend to, but buy one at the market!), everyone in sight will congratulate you, as well as advise you how to cook and eat your catch. Need a recipe? The simplest method is to simmer the squid in its own ink. Otherwise, hang it up on a line until the sun completely dries it out (at least 12 hours), cut it up into very thin slices, grill it over open coals, and then sprinkle it with lemon juice. For something along the same lines but not quite so esoteric, try a dish of *calamares*, or deep-fried squid, in a local restaurant.

Sobrasada: a typical Balearic dish of pork sausage with sweet peppers.

Dulces: **sweets**, the great Ibiza weakness, from typical Balearic sweet breakfast rolls (*ensaimadas*) to *graixonera*, a kind of bread pudding, and *flaó*, a tart made with fresh goat's cheese and mint. Even *macarrones de San Juan* turn out to be noodles cooked in sweetened milk flavoured with cinnamon.

Local **fruit** is delicious, and the fresh produce of Ibiza will jolt your palate awake. After a large lunch on a hot day, try a bunch of grapes from the nearby vines, cooling in a bowl of water, a fat, juicy peach, or a ripe melon.

A beaming chef and his breaded mackerel that would bring a smile to anyone's face.

In the right season, abandon any weight concerns and tuck into a bowl of fresh strawberries and cream (*fresas con nata*), widely advertised by the island's restaurants and cafés.

Restaurants and Meal Times

Spanish restaurants are officially graded and then awarded a number of forks: one fork is the lowest, four forks the élite. Note that ratings are awarded according to facilities, however, and not to the quality of the food, several forks may only guarantee higher prices.

Café culture on Ibiza: find a table and peruse, chat, mingle, and just give yourself over to it all.

A good way to choose a restaurant is to have a look in and check how many Ibicencos and deeply tanned expatriates are eating there. If a lot of these value-conscious, knowledgeable customers are there, then chances are you've found the right place to get a satisfying meal no matter what the official rating is.

Spanish restaurants generally offer a "day's special" (*menú del día*). This is normally three courses plus wine at a set price. The *menú* proves economical if not inspired, since

Enjoy your meal!
¡Buen provecho!
(bwayn pro**vaych**oh)

the law stipulates that the price charged cannot be more than 80 per cent of the à la carte sum of its parts. It is important to note that if a waiter asks "*Menú?*," he is referring to the special dish of the day. If you want to look at the actual menu and see what else is offered, then you should ask for "*la carta*."

Most menu prices include taxes and a service charge, but it's customary to leave a tip if you were served satisfactorily. Around 10 per cent is usually the appropriate amount. All restaurants announce that official complaint forms are available to dissatisfied clients.

On the Spanish mainland, late dining hours perplex visitors. Lunch hardly ever seems to start until 2:00 P.M., and dinner may wait till 10:00 P.M. However, on Ibiza the farmer-and-fisherman tradition rules out late meals. Restaurants serve lunch from 1:00 to 3:00 P.M. and dinner from about 8:00 to 11:00 P.M.

One useful hint for keeping costs down: ask for *vino de la casa* (house wine)—it'll cost well under half the price of a brand wine, and offer tolerable quality into the bargain. Overall, most drinks are less expensive than in the U.K. and U.S.

Breakfast, Anyone?

While lunch and dinner may be major meals, the standard Ibizan breakfast is simply a cup of coffee and a pastry. *Ensaimadas*—sweet rolls made with lard—are a Balearic speciality generally available on the island. In winter you can sample *churros*, sugared fritters, that you dip into coffee or hot chocolate.

Pastries are irresistible wherever you go —these are some of the delectable nibbles available.

In deference to foreign habits, most hotels and some cafés now offer a *desayuno completo* consisting of orange juice, toast, and coffee, either with or without eggs. Breakfast coffee (*café con leche*) is half coffee, half hot milk.

Hot chocolate with cream is known as *un suizo*, meaning, not illogically, "a Swiss."

Beach Restaurants

For drinks and snacks at the water's edge, there's nothing like a beach restaurant. These modest establishments are set up right on the sand. Because they're supposed to be dismantled at the end of each season, most are somewhat makeshift, but they are nonetheless convenient and appealingly strong on atmosphere.

Bars and Cafés

From early in the morning to late at night, bars and cafés serve breakfast, snacks, coffee, and drinks. Open-air cafés are one of the area's pleasures. A cup of coffee buys you a ringside seat for as long as you care to linger; no one will rush you. The sole exception is in Sant Antoni, where some cafés refuse to serve coffee at all during peak hours, preferring the high profits from alcohol.

> **You're welcome! -**
> *De nada.* (day nahdah)

Wines and spirits are served at all hours in Spain. Children are welcome in most bars and often accompany their parents on late-night outings, having recouped their energy during their siesta.

Bar and café bills include service, but small tips are the custom. It usually costs 20 percent less to sit at the bar for a coffee or a drink than being served at a table.

Note that *cafeterías* aren't self-service restaurants as you may know them, but are glorified snack bars. The word orig-

A cup of coffee ordered at one of Ibiza's open-air cafés (except in Sant Antoni) allows one to linger indefinitely.

inally meant a café, but service has been expanded to include full meals at quite high prices.

Bodegas are "wine cellars." On the mainland, many popular tourist bars have been designed to re-create the feel of a traditional wine cellar. However, on Ibiza, a *bodega* is usually a wholesale and retail wine store rather than a place to sit and try the vintages. Prices are reasonable here.

Tapas

A *tapa* is a bite-sized morsel of food—meatballs, olives, fried fish tidbits, shellfish, vegetable salad; it can be almost anything edible. The word itself, *tapa*, is translated as "lid" and derives from the old custom of offering a bite of food along with a drink, the food being served on a saucer sitting on top of the glass like a lid. Nowadays, sadly, the custom of giving away the *tapa* is nonexistent, though the idea of selling snacks is stronger than ever. Some bars specialize in them. Instead of sitting down to a formal meal in a restaurant you can wander into a *tapas* bar, point to the items you like and eat your way down the counter, rather like a smorgasbord. Usually *tapas* include seafood, meatballs, salad vegetables, fried fish, and olives. One helping is called a *porción*, a large serving is a *ración*, half as much a *media-ración*. It pays to learn these terms, as it's quite possible to spend more for *tapas* than for a conventional dinner.

Wines and Spirits

The most famous of all Spanish wines is, of course, **Sherry** (*vino de Jerez*), a wine fortified with brandy. You will find two principal types: *fino* and *oloroso*. *Fino* is a dry Sherry, pale in colour with a rich bouquet. In this category belong *manzanillas* and *amontillados*. Any *fino* will make a good aperitif.

An *oloroso*, on the other hand, is a heavy, dark dessert wine, which is sweetened before being sold. Brown and cream Sherries are *olorosos*, and so is an *amoroso*, though it's medium dry and pale in colour. An *oloroso* is a good after-dinner drink.

For an adequate **table wine**, try one of the many unpretentious wines that come from mainland Spain or Mallorca.

Quenching a Thirst

In the Balearics, wine is often drunk from a communal container made of pottery or glass and known as a *porrón*. With its wide mouth and long, tapering spout, this looks more like a watering can than a drinking vessel. You fill it at the top and drink from the spout; the stylized shape is traditional. The version for water, drunk the same way, is called a *cántaro*; during the heat of the day workmen will pass this round so that everyone present can drink their fill.

The technique isn't easy to master. Tilt the container until the liquid flows into your mouth in a stream, and don't touch the spout with your lips or tongue.

Legend credits the Moors with its invention. Apparently they were inspired—so the story goes—by the Prophet's dictum that wine should not be allowed to touch Muslim lips.

These unsung, yet worthy, vintages very often cost hardly any more than bottled mineral water. In contrast, some of the well-known Spanish wines are overpriced and not necessarily of better quality.

¡A su salud!
-Cheers!

On rare occasions you may find a restaurant serving *vino de pagés* (local red wine). Islanders often drink the somewhat acid wine mixed with lemonade (*gaseosa*).

If you're not in the mood for wine with your meal, have no qualms about ordering something else instead. No one will turn up a snobbish nose if you prefer beer, mineral water, or a soft drink. In fact, at lunchtime even some Ibicencos themselves consider wine off-limits—it's just too relaxing.

Spanish **brandy** has a less delicate taste than French Cognac, and you may find it too heavy or sweet for your liking. It's very cheap, though—often the same price as a soft drink. An expensive brand like *Carlos I* is much smoother.

Sangría, rather like punch, is a popular thirst-quenching refresher, especially in summer. Made from a mixture of red wine, lemon and orange juice and peel, brandy, and mineral water with ice, it may strike you as too heavy to be consumed with a meal. Whenever you do try it, make certain it's freshly made.

A word about **prices**. If you insist on sticking to imported Scotch or Bourbon, expect to pay a relative fortune. However, a wide range of familiar liquors and liqueurs are available at very low prices made under licence in Spain. A visit to a large liquor store will reveal prices startlingly lower than what you'd pay at home.

Ibiza is mildly famous for its own native **liqueurs**. The most widely seen is *hierbas* (which means, literally, herbs). This sweet and fairly mild potion is by and large a homemade product that is blended with herbs and sold in old bottles. It costs less, and may taste better, in the remote areas.

A winery displays its indigenous products. Alcoholic beverages are abundant on Ibiza and Formentera.

The syrupy *hierbas* (YAIR-bass) may be sipped before or after meals. In hot weather, the locals drink it with ice.

Frigola, a sweet, digestive drink good with ice, is commercially bottled in Ibiza from formulas using island-grown herbs. Two aromatic aniseed drinks are also produced locally. Beware though, since these colourless liquids have a considerable kick. *Anís dulce* is sweet; *anís seco,* dry and dangerously potent. It resembles French *pastis*, Greek *ouzo,* or Turkish *raki*. Ibizans like their *anís* neat (straight). Foreign imbibers, not brought up on this custom, usually prefer to dilute it with a large splash of water. *Palo*, a slightly bitter aniseed drink dark brown in colour, tastes best in a long tall glass with the addition of gin or soda and ice.

To help you order and for more information on wining and dining in Ibiza, we would recommend you purchase the Berlitz Spanish-English/English-Spanish PHRASE BOOK AND DICTIONARY or the Berlitz EUROPEAN MENU READER.

To Help You Order ...

Could we have a table?	**¿Nos puede dar una mesa?**
Do you have a set menu?	**¿Tiene un menú del día?**
I'd like a/an/some ...	**Quisiera ...**

beer	**una cerveza**	milk	**leche**
bread	**pan**	mineral water	**agua mineral**
coffee	**un café**	napkin	**una servilleta**
cutlery	**los cubiertos**	salad	**una ensalada**
fish	**pescado**	sandwich	**un bocadillo**
fruit	**fruta**	sugar	**azúcar**
glass	**un vaso**	tea	**un té**
meat	**carne**	(iced) water	**agua (fresca)**
menu	**la carta**	wine	**vino**

... and Read the Menu

albóndigas	**meatballs**	lenguado	**sole**
almejas	**baby clams**	manzana	**apple**
anchoas	**anchovies**	mariscos	**shellfish**
angulas	**baby eels**	mejillones	**mussels**
arroz	**rice**	melocotón	**peach**
atún	**tunny (tuna)**	merluza	**hake**
bacalao	**codfish**	naranja	**orange**
besugo	**sea bream**	pescadilla	**whiting**
boquerones	**fresh anchovies**	pez espada	**swordfish**
caballa	**mackerel**	pimiento	**green pepper**
cerdo	**pork**	piña	**pineapple**
chorizo	**a spicy pork**	plátano	**banana**
	sausage	pollo	**chicken**
cordero	**lamb**	postre	**dessert**
dorada	**sea bass**	pulpo	**octopus**
entremeses	**hors-d'oeuvre**	queso	**cheese**
filete	**filet**	salchichón	**salami**

INDEX

HANDY TRAVEL TIPS

An A–Z Summary of Practical Information

A

ACCOMMODATION *(hotel; alojamiento)* (See also CAMPING on page 102 and the list of RECOMMENDED HOTELS starting on page 129)

Spanish hotel prices are no longer government controlled. Accommodation in the Balearics ranges from the simple but clean rooms in a *pensión* (boarding house) to the more luxurious surroundings of a resort hotel. The majority of visitors to Ibiza favour travel with a package tour, so accommodation will be arranged in advance, but if you're travelling independently, when you check in you will be asked to sign a form indicating the hotel category, room number, and price (which usually includes breakfast). Off-season rates are theoretically lower, and vacancies, of course, are much more numerous.

One of the most popular types of accommodation is a package arrangement consisting of a furnished apartment or villa. The cost is often little more than the scheduled airfare alone, but arrangements usually have to be made well in advance.

Hotel-residencia and hostal. With a few luxurious exceptions, these are modest hotels, often family concerns. They are also graded by stars (one to three).

Pensión. Boarding house with few amenities.

a single/double room	**una habitación sencilla/doble**
with bath/shower	**con bano/ducha**
What's the rate per night?	**¿Cuál es el precio por noche?**
Is there a reduction for children?	**¿Hay algún descuento para los niños?**
That's too expensive.	**Eso es demasiado caro.**

AIRPORT *(aeropuerto)*

Both international and domestic services fly into Ibiza's modern airport. Porters are always available to carry your bags the few steps to the taxi rank or bus stop. Souvenir shops, tourist information offices, car hire, and currency-exchange counters operate here, as well as a duty-free shop. (Ordinary shops in the towns sell perfume, tobacco, and alcohol, tax included, at reasonable prices.) Airline buses link the airport with the centre of Ibiza Town, a 15-minute drive. There is a bus service every half hour between roughly 7am and 10am.

Porter!	**¡Mozo!**
Taxi!	**¡Taxi!**
Where's the bus for …?	**¿Dónde está el autobús para …?**

B

BICYCLE and MOTORSCOOTER HIRE *(bicicletas/scooters de alquiler)* (See also DRIVING on page 107)

A practical and fun way to explore the islands is to hire two-wheeled transportation which can cope with even the most narrow and bumpy paths. Bicycles may often be hired from the same places that offer motorscooters and mopeds, but at about one-quarter the price. A drivers licence is required when renting a vespa or a mobylette.

Vespas are squat motorscooters of 150 to 175 cc, powerful enough to transport driver and passenger with ease. Mobylettes are more elementary, 49 cc mopeds requiring little mechanical knowledge. Passengers are not permitted and maximum speed is about 30 km (18½ miles) per hour. For more adventurous speedsters, Bultaco trail bikes (250 cc) are occasionally available.

The use of crash helmets is compulsory in Spain when driving a motorcycle, whatever the capacity of the engine.

Where can we hire mountain bikes?	**¿Dónde alquilan bicis de montaña?**
I'd like to hire a bicycle.	**Quisiera alquilar una bicicleta.**

Ibiza and Formentera

What's the charge per day/week?	**¿Cuánto cobran por día/semana?**

C

CAMPING *(camping)*

On Ibiza, you can camp at sites near Sant Antoni (off Ibiza Town road), at Cala Bassa (west of Sant Antoni), at Cala Llonga, Punta Arabí, and Es Canar (all of which are near Santa Eulària), and at Cala de Portinatx up on the north coast.

Less demanding wanderers have been known to set up camp in Ibiza's coastal caves. If you sleep out in the open, don't stay too close to camping and caravan (trailer) sites. Police responsible for the campsite may awaken you to check identity.

On Formentera camping is prohibited.

May we camp here?	**¿Podemos acampar aquí?**
We have a tent/caravan (trailer).	**Tenemos una tienda de camping/una caravana.**

CAR HIRE *(coches de alquiler)* (See also DRIVING on page 107 and MONEY MATTERS on page 117)

Car-hire firms in Ibiza handle a wide variety of cars, the few automatics that are available being disproportionately expensive. The rates vary accordingly, and off-season rates are often lower.

General conditions for hire include a refundable deposit plus 20% of the estimated rental charge paid in advance. Major credit cards offer a preferable alternative to giving a cash deposit. There's also a VAT or sales tax on total rental charges. Third-party insurance is automatically included; for an extra fee the customer may have full insurance coverage.

Renting a car for the day usually means from 8am to 8am. Fuel (and traffic fines) are the customer's responsibility. Visitors from overseas should in theory have an International Driving Permit, but American licences are accepted almost everywhere. European visitors do not need an International Permit if they have a pink European Driving Licence.

I'd like to rent a car tomorrow.	**Quisiera alquilar un coche para mañana.**
for one day/a week	**por un día/una semana**
Please include full insurance	**Haga el favor de incluir el seguro a todo riesgo.**

CLIMATE and CLOTHING

Ibiza is blessed with a relatively mild climate throughout the year. Maximum temperatures in winter, however, can be a bit cooler than in many other Spanish resorts, and even in the summer months when the weather is at its warmest, the nights can turn chilly, so it's best to go prepared with a sweater or light jacket. Similarly, though rain is the exception rather than the rule in summer, it can catch visitors unaware. A pack-away raincoat or umbrella is a good investment.

Ibiza enjoys a yearly average of 300 days of sunshine with a daily mean of five hours in winter and more than ten hours in summer. Humidity is about 70% most of the year, rising to a high 85% in August.

Because the winter climate can be somewhat unpredictable, package tours during this season are cheaper than in the summer, and you'll find the resorts much quieter (though service can suffer as a result). The chart below shows monthly averages for Ibiza.

	J	F	M	A	M	J	J	A	S	O	N	D
Air temperature												
°F	54	53	56	59	63	71	77	79	72	68	61	56
°C	12	12	13	15	17	22	25	26	22	20	16	13
Water temperature												
°F	56	57	57	61	67	71	76	80	73	68	65	61
°C	13	14	14	16	20	21	24	26	22	20	18	16
Days of sunshine	26	14	21	15	28	28	27	31	28	19	24	28

Clothing. Given Ibiza's reputation for freewheeling tolerance, it would be surprising if anyone laid down rules. Dress is informal, ranging from discreet to outlandish. As is the case everywhere else, good taste is the ultimate rule.

When you're packing, don't fail to consider the calendar. In July and August you're unlikely to need anything beyond the lightest summer clothing, day or night. At any other time of year — even when it's blistering hot at midday — you may have to dress warmer for cool night breezes. In the hot weather, cotton is preferable to — and more comfortable than — synthetic fabrics.

On the beach, dressing poses less of a problem. Some people wear nothing at all (there's official nude bathing in certain areas) and many women go topless.

When you're walking to or from the beach, shirts or informal dresses are recommended to be worn on top of swimsuits; the same goes for town wear. More sober clothing should, as a matter of courtesy, be worn when visiting churches. Don't put on a swimsuit or shorts, for example.

COMMUNICATIONS (See also OPENING HOURS on page 119 and TIME DIFFERENCES on page 123)

Post offices (*correos*). Post offices are used for mail and telegrams only; you can't usually make telephone calls from them. Some of them limit acceptance of registered mail to certain times, and they often stay open a few hours after the normal closing for telegraph business. Mail boxes are yellow with red stripes.

Parcels (*paquetes*) up to 2 kilograms (4.4 pounds) can be mailed from local post offices. Heavier parcels must be sent from the main post office in Ibiza Town.

If you don't know ahead of time where you'll be staying, you can have your mail addressed to *lista de correos* (poste restante or general delivery) at whichever town is most convenien. For example:

Mr. John Smith
Lista de Correos
Sant Antoni Abad
Ibiza (Baleares)
Spain

Take your passport with you to the post office for identification.

Telegrams (*telegramas*). The main post office in Ibiza Town handles telegrams from 9am to 1:30am and 3 to 8am daily; branches are only open 9am to 2am. Your hotel desk will also take care of telegrams for you. Night-letters or night-rate telegrams (*telegrama de noche*) are delivered the following morning and cost less than straight-rate messages.

Telephones (*teléfono*). Ibiza's automatic dialling system allows you to dial numbers throughout Spain. However, it's often impossible to reach a number across town. Coins of 5, 25, and 100 pesetas should be lined up on the ledge before dialling. Unused coins will be returned.

Overseas calls can be made from your hotel (the most expensive way), or more cheaply from telephone offices or call boxes. Be sure to have enough change to complete your call, as these public telephones have no numbers and the other party cannot ring you back. For international direct dialling, pick up the receiver, wait for the dial tone, then dial 07; wait for a second sound and dial the country code, city code, and subscriber's number.

To reverse the charges, ask for *cobro revertido*. For a personal (person-to-person) call, specify *persona a persona*.

To find a telephone number for Ibiza Town in the island directory, look under the town's Ibicenco name, Eivissa.

Have you received any mail for me?	**¿Ha recibido correo para mí?**
A stamp for this letter/postcard, please.	**Por favor, un sello para esta carta/targeta postal.**
express (special delivery)	**urgente**
airmail	**vía aérea**
registered	**certificado**
I want to send a telegram to …	**Quisiera mandar un telegrama a …**
Can you get me this number in …?	**¿Puede communi-carme con este número en …?**

COMPLAINTS (*reclamación*)

Tourism is Spain's leading industry, and the government takes complaints from tourists very seriously.

Ibiza and Formentera

Hotels, campsites, and restaurants. By law, all hotels, campsites, and restaurants must maintain a supply of official complaint forms (*Hoja Oficial de Reclamación/Full Oficial de Reclamació*) accessible to guests. The original of this triplicate document should be sent to the regional office of the Ministry of Tourism; one copy stays with the establishment against which the complaint is registered, while the final copy remains in your hands as a record. Merely asking for this is usually enough of a threat to resolve most matters.

New legislation has been introduced that greatly strengthens the consumer's hand. Public information offices are being set up, controls carried out, and fallacious information made punishable by law. For a tourist's needs, however, the tourist office or, in really serious cases, the police would normally be able to handle it or, at least, advise where to go.

CRIME *(crimen, robo)* (See also EMERGENCIES on page 111 and POLICE on page 120)

Unfortunately, even on a small island like Ibiza, there has been an upsurge in petty thievery. In crowded places like markets, tourists should be on the lookout for pickpockets and bag-snatchers. Don't under any circumstances take any valuables to the beach, or leave them open to view in the car.

I want to report a theft.   **Quiero denunciar un robo.**

CUSTOMS and ENTRY FORMALITIES

Most visitors, including citizens of Great Britain, the U.S.A., Canada, Ireland, Australia, and New Zealand, require only a valid passport — no visa, no health certificate — to enter Spain. If in doubt, check with your travel agent before departure.

The formalities at Ibiza airport are generally so informal that passports aren't even stamped. You're usually entitled to stay in Spain for up to 90 days. If you expect to remain longer, a Spanish consulate or tourist office can advise you.

The severely uniformed, white-gloved Spanish customs officials may or may not ask you to open your suitcase for inspection. If you are stopped for any reason, honesty and courtesy should help move procedures along quickly.

Duty free: As Spain is part of the EU, free exchange of non–duty free-goods for personal use is permitted between Ibiza and the U.K. and Ireland. However, duty-free items are still subject to restrictions: check before you go. For residents of non-EU countries, restrictions are as follows: **Australia**: 250 cigarettes **or** 250g tobacco; 1*l* alcohol; **Canada**: 200 cigarettes **and** 50 cigars **and** 400g tobacco; 1.14*l* spirits **or** wine **or** 8.5*l* beer; **New Zealand**: 200 cigarettes **or** 50 cigars **or** 250g tobacco; 4.5*l* wine **or** beer **and** 1.1*l* spirits; **South Africa**: 400 cigarettes **and** 50 cigars **and** 250g tobacco; 2*l* wine **and** 1*l* spirits; **U.S.A.**: 200 cigarettes **and** 100 cigars **or** a "reasonable amount" of tobacco.

Currency restrictions. Tourists may bring an unlimited amount of Spanish or foreign currency into the country. Departing, though, you must declare any amount beyond the equivalent of 500,000 pesetas. Thus if you plan to carry large sums in and out again it's wise to declare your currency on arrival as well as on departure.

I've nothing to declare.	**No tengo nada que declarar.**
It's for my personal use.	**Es para mi uso personal.**

D

DRIVING

To take your car into Spain, you should have: an International Driving Permit (not obligatory for most Western European citizens — ask your automobile association — but recommended in case of difficulties with the police as it carries a text in Spanish) or a legalized and certified translation of your driver's licence; car registration papers; and a Green Card (an extension of your regular insurance policy, making it valid for foreign countries).

Also recommended: with your certificate of insurance, you should carry a bail bond. If you injure somebody in an accident in Spain, you can be imprisoned while the accident is under investigation. This bond will bail you out. Apply for one from your automobile association or insurance company.

Driving conditions on Ibiza. The rules are the same as in mainland Spain and the rest of the Continent: drive on the right, pass on the left, yield right of way to all vehicles coming from the right. Spanish drivers tend to use their horn when passing. If your car has seat belts, it's obligatory to use them; fines for noncompliance are high.

The roads of Ibiza are a few years behind the times. Except for the Sant Antoni-Ibiza motorway and other main thoroughfares, they're narrow, twisting, filled with potholes, and badly signposted. Be warned that quaint local attractions — such as horse-drawn carts, donkeys, sheep, and goats — can become deadly perils on the road. When passing through villages, drive with extra care.

Other hazards to look out for include loose gravel and sand on the roadway. (The latter can be as slippery as ice.) Give plenty of leeway to motorbikes, scooters, and bicycles. Never pass any vehicle or obstruction without signalling.

Speed limits on the islands are 100kph (62 mph) or 90 km/h (56 mph) on the open road and 60 km/h (37 mph) in built-up areas. The speed limit for cars towing caravans/trailers 80 km/h (50 mph).

Traffic police. The armed Civil Guard (*Guardia Civil*) patrol the few highways of Ibiza by car and on powerful motorcycles. Always in pairs, these tough-looking *hombres* are courteous and will stop to help anyone in trouble. They're also severe on lawbreakers.

If you receive a fine, you will be expected to pay it on the spot. The most common offences include passing without directional-indicator lights flashing, travelling too close to the car in front, and travelling with a burned-out head- or taillight. (Spanish law shrewdly requires you to carry a spare bulb at all times.)

Parking. In Ibiza Town, Sant Antoni, and Santa Eulària, the traffic police have become much stricter about incorrect parking, and cars are either towed away to the police pound (behind avinguda Isidoro Macabich) or clamped and immobilized. To remove the clamp can be a time-consuming process.

In the case of the *cepo* (clamp), a notice is placed on the windshield warning the motorist not to drive because irreparable damage may occur to the car. In the case of both the *cepo* and towing away, a fine must be paid.

Fuel and oil. All service stations are obliged by law to sell each grade of fuel at the same price. Not every station has a choice of fuels at a given time, and it is recommended that you buy only the best grade available.

There are not that many service stations on the island so be sure not to run too low on fuel. Petrol (gasoline) station hours are completely irregular at weekends and during fiestas (the local publication, *Diario de Ibiza* — see page 116 — carries a listing of stations that remain open), and motorists may have to go from Santa Eulària to Sant Josép for petrol on a Sunday. The local rule is: always fill up on a Friday and before a fiesta, as well as before nightfall in the summer, when usually only one station stays open on the whole island.

Breakdowns. Because of the heavy workload and a shortage of qualified mechanics, repairs may take longer than they would at home. Spare parts are readily available for Spanish-built cars, but the spares of other makes may be very difficult to obtain.

Road signs. Most road signs are the standard pictographs used throughout Europe. However, you may encounter these written signs:

Aparcamiento	Parking
Atención	Caution
Baches	Pot-holes
Blandones	Soft shoulders
Bordes deteriorados	Deteriorated road edges
Ceda el paso	Give way (Yield)
Despacio	Slow
Desviación	Diversion (Detour)
Escuela	School
Estacionamento prohibido/ Prohibido aparcar	No parking

Ibiza and Formentera

Obras	Road works
¡Pare!	Stop
Peatones	Pedestrians
Peligro	Danger
Puesto de socorro	First-aid post
Salida de camiones	Lorry (Truck) exit
(International) Driver's Licence	**carné de conducir (internacional)**
car registration papers	**permiso de circulación**
Green Card	**Carta Verde**
Are we on the right road for …?	**¿Es ésta la carretera hacia …?**
Fill the tank please, top grade.	**Llénelo, por favor, con super.**
Check the oil/tyres/battery.	**Por favor, controle el aceite/los neu-máticos/la batería.**
I've had a breakdown.	**Mi coche se ha estropeado.**
There's been an accident.	**Ha habido un accidente.**

Fluid measures

Distance

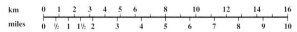

ELECTRIC CURRENT *(corriente eléctrica)*
Both 125 and 220 volt, 50c (AC) are used on the island. To play it safe, ask at your hotel desk.

Occasionally, especially when it rains, there is a brief blackout. No one has explained why, but some think it adds to the island's romantic mood. Most hotels supply a candle in every room.

What's the voltage — 125 or 220?	**¿Cuál es el voltaje — ciento veinti-cinco (125) o doscientos veinte (220)?**
an adapter	**un adaptador**
a battery	**una pila**

EMBASSIES and CONSULATES *(consulado)*
Almost all western European countries have consular offices on Ibiza and Majorca, or in Barcelona. All embassies are located in Madrid. If you run into trouble with the authorities or the police, consult your consulate for advice.

British vice-consulate: Avinguda Isidoro Macabich, 45, Ibiza Town; tel. 30 18 18.

French vice-consulate: Vare de Rey, 18, Ibiza Town; tel. 31 51 11.

German vice-consulate: Carrer d'Antoni Jaume, 2, Ibiza Town; tel. 31 57 63.

Irish consulate: Gran Via Carles III, 94, Barcelona; tel. 3 30 96 52.

U.S. consulate: Via Laietana, 33, Barcelona; tel. 3 19 95 50.

Where's the British/American consulate?	**¿Dónde está el consulado británico/americano?**
It's very urgent.	**Es muy urgente.**
I need to make an urgent telephone call.	**Necesito hacer una llamada urgente.**

EMERGENCIES *(urgencia)* (See also EMBASSIES on page 111, MEDICALCARE on page 116, and POLICE on page 120)

If your hotel desk clerk isn't able to help, here are a couple of pertinent telephone numbers:

Police Emergency	**091**
Ambulance	**30 12 14**
Fire	**31 30 30**

G

GAY and LESBIAN TRAVELLERS

Spain is a popular place with gay and lesbian travellers, and few places more so than Ibiza. The island has a host of bars, clubs, cafés, restaurants, and hotels and vacation apartments aimed specifically at gay tourists. This is truly a place to relax and have fun.

GUIDES and INTERPRETERS *(guía, intérprete)* (See also TOURIST INFORMATION OFFICES on page 123)

Local tourist offices can direct you to qualified guides and interpreters and will also inform you of the general price range. In most centres, an English-speaking guide can be hired at short notice.

We'd like an English speaking guide.	**Queremos un guía que hable inglés.**
I need an English interpreter.	**Necesito un intérprete de inglés.**

L

LANGUAGE

Castilian, the national language of Spain, is understood everywhere. However, the islanders customarily communicate among themselves in Ibicenco, derived from the Catalan language. Since Castilian is, in effect, not the local language for the residents, they may speak it more slowly than mainland Spaniards do. English and French are useful backup languages in tourist areas. On a brief visit to Ibiza it would be difficult to learn a lot of the local version of Catalan. Nonetheless, a few words of Ibicenco dialect will go a long way in producing a smile and friendship. You can always rely on the all-purpose Spanish expression, "*es igual.*" Said with a shrug, it can mean anything from "you're welcome" to "who cares?"

Ibicenco	English	Castilian
Bon dia	Good morning	**Buenos días**
Bones tardes	Good afternoon	**Buenas tardes**
Bona nit	Good night	**Buenas noches**

Gràcies	Thank you	**Gracias**
De res	You're welcome	**De nada**
Per favor	Please	**Por favor**
Adéu	Goodbye	**Adiós**

NUMBERS

0	cero	12	doce	31	treinta y uno
1	uno	13	trece	32	treinta y dos
2	dos	14	catorce	40	cuarenta
3	tres	15	quince	50	cincuenta
4	cuatro	16	dieciséis	60	sesenta
5	cinco	17	diecisiete	70	sesenta
6	seis	18	dieciocho	80	ochenta
7	siete	19	diecinueve	90	noventa
8	ocho	20	veinte	100	cien
9	nueve	21	veintiuno	101	ciento uno
10	diez	22	veintidós	500	quinientos
11	once	30	treinta	1,000	mil

The Berlitz SPANISH PHRASE BOOK AND DICTIONARY covers most situations you're likely to encounter in your travels in Spain. In addition, the Berlitz SPANISH-ENGLISH/ENGLISH-SPANISH POCKET DICTIONARY contains a 12,500-word glossary of each language, plus a menu-reader supplement.

SOME USEFUL EXPRESSIONS

where/when/how	**dónde/cuándo/cómo**
how long/how far	**cuànto tiempo/a qué distancia**
yesterday/today/tomorrow	**ayer/hoy/mañana**
day/week/month/year	**día/semana/mes/año**
left/right	**izquierda/derecha**
up/down	**arriba/bajo**
good/bad	**bueno/malo**
big/small	**grande/pequeño**

Ibiza and Formentera

cheap/expensive	**barato/caro**
hot/cold	**caliente/frío**
old/new	**viejo/nuevo**
open/closed	**abierto/cerrado**
here/there	**aquí/allí**
free (vacant)/occupied	**libre/ocupado**
early/late	**temprano/tarde**
easy/difficult	**fácil/difícil**
What does this mean?	**¿Qué quiere decir esto?**
Please write it down.	**Por favor, escríbalo.**
Is there an admission charge?	**¿Se debe pagar la entrada?**
I'd like …	**Quisiera …**
Have you something less expensive?	**¿Tiene algo más barato?**
Just a minute.	**Un momento.**
Get a doctor, quickly!	**¡Llamen a un médico, ràpidamente!**

LAUNDRY and DRY-CLEANING (*lavandería; tintorería*)

Most hotels will handle laundry and dry-cleaning, but they usually charge more than a public laundry (*lavandería*) or a dry cleaner (*tintorería*). You'll find do-it-yourself launderettes in a few areas.

I must have this for tomorrow morning.	**Lo necesito para mañana por la mañana.**

LOST PROPERTY (*objetos perdidos*)

If you lose something, check first at your hotel desk, then report the loss to the municipal police or *Guardia Civil* (Civil Guard).

If you lose track of a child at a beach, you should first inquire at the nearest beach bar or restaurant. In town, a lost child would most likely be taken to the municipal police station or Civil Guard barracks.

I've lost my wallet/handbag.   **He perdido mi cartera/bolso.**

M

MAPS and STREET NAMES

On Ibiza and Formentera, some places have two names, one Castilian, another Ibicenco — a situation that often puzzles tourists. To add to the confusion, maps aren't always consistent in their use of place names. With the upsurge in regional consciousness that has been ongoing since the death of Franco, place names have become something of a bone of contention here, as elsewhere in Spain, and some Ibiza people would like to see all Castilian place names changed to their Ibicenco equivalents. Within towns and villages the words for "street," "square," and so on have been changed from Castilian to Ibicenco, and when new streets are created they are given Ibicenco names (see also page 115).

a street plan of …   **un plano de la ciudad de …**

a road map of the island   **un mapa de carreteras de la isla**

MEDIA

Newspapers and magazines (*periódico; revista*). During the height of the tourist season, all major British and Continental newspapers are on sale in Ibiza on the evening of their publication day or the following morning. European and U.S. magazines are always available, as is the Paris-based *International Herald Tribune*. For additional news, the local *Ibiza News,* aimed at English-speaking tourists, is published weekly.

If you can read a bit of Spanish, you might also be interested in the daily *Diario de Ibiza*, the local tabloid daily.

Do you have any English-   **¿Tienen periódicos en inglés?**
language newspapers?

Radio and television (*radio; televisión*). Most hotels have television lounges, but all programmes are broadcast in Spanish.

Travellers with short-wave radios will be able to pick up the BBC World Service and the Voice of America very clearly at night and in the early morning. Ibiza's local commercial radio stations have programmes in English and German, at least during the summer season, and one station also broadcasts in French and Italian.

MEDICAL CARE

The most common cause of illness amongst tourists on Ibiza is an excess of sun, food, or alcohol — or a combination of all three. The motto to remember is moderation.

To be completely at ease, make certain your health insurance policy covers any illness or accident while on holiday. Before leaving home, British citizens should apply at any main post office for form E111, which gives a reciprocal health care agreement between the U.K. and Spain. Your travel agent can also fix you up with Spanish tourist insurance (ASTES), but it is a slow-moving process. This covers doctor's fees and clinical care in the event of emergency.

Do your eyes a favour and wear sunglasses. You may never have seen the sun so brightly and glaringly reflected off white walls.

Note that no Ibiza beaches maintain a lifeguard.

There are doctors in the towns on Ibiza, and their consulting hours are posted. For less serious matters, first-aid personnel, called *practicantes*, may be consulted. Some *practicantes* make daily rounds of the major tourist hotels, just in case.

Hospitals. There are a number of outpatient clinics on the island, and one of them operates round the clock in Ibiza Town. In the event of grave emergency, your hotel staff would probably send you there.

Pharmacies/drugstores (*farmacias*) are usually open during shopping hours. After hours, one shop in each town is always on duty for emergencies. Its address is posted daily at all the other chemists.

a dentist	**un dentista**
a doctor	**un médico**
an ambulance	**una ambulancia**
hospital	**hospital**
an upset stomach	**molestias de estómago**

sunstroke	**una insolación**
Get a doctor, quickly!	**¡Llamen a un médico, rápidamente!**

MONEY MATTERS

Currency. The monetary unit of Spain is the *peseta* (its abbreviated form is written *pta*).

Coins: 1, 5, 10, 25, 50, 100, 200, and 500 pesetas.

Banknotes: 1,000, 2,000, 5,000, and 10,000 pesetas.

A 5 peseta coin is traditionally called a *duro*, so if a price is quoted as 10 duros, it means 50 pesetas.

Exchange Offices. Outside normal banking hours (see Opening Hours on page 120), many travel agencies and other businesses displaying a "*cambio*" sign will change foreign currency into pesetas. The exchange rate is a bit less favourable than in the banks. Both banks and exchange offices pay slightly more for traveller's cheques than for cash. Always take your passport with you for identification when you go to change money.

Credit cards. All the internationally recognized cards are accepted by hotels, restaurants, and businesses in Spain.

Eurocheques. You'll have no problem settling bills or paying for purchases with Eurocheques.

Traveller's cheques. In tourist areas, shops, banks, hotels, and travel agencies accept traveller's cheques, though you're likely to get a better exchange rate at a national or regional bank. Remember you need your passport if you expect to cash a traveller's cheque.

Paying cash. Although many shops and bars will accept payment in sterling or dollars, you're better off paying in pesetas. Shops will invariably give you less than the bank rate for foreign currency.

Where's the nearest bank/currency exchange office?	**¿Dónde está el banco/la oficina de cambio más cercana?**
I want to change some pounds/dollars.	**Quiero cambiar unas libras/unos dólares.**

Ibiza and Formentera

Do you accept traveller's cheques?	**¿Acepta usted cheques de viaje?**
Can I pay with this credit card?	**¿Puedo pagar con esta tarjeta de crédito?**

PLANNING YOUR BUDGET

Because of Ibiza's tourist boom — and because it's an island — certain prices tend to be higher than on mainland Spain. However, the cost of living still remains lower than in many other European countries and in North America.

How much your holiday will cost depends upon your budget and taste, but you really don't need a lot of money to have a good time in Spain. Some prices seem topsy-turvy. In a neighbourhood bar, soft drinks, beer, and Spanish brandy all cost about the same, but a bottle of mineral water may cost more than a bottle of wine. Generally, the biggest bargains are in the realm of eating, drinking, and smoking.

To give you an idea of what to expect, here are some average prices in Spanish pesetas. However, they should be regarded as approximate, as inflation creeps relentlessly up. Prices quoted may be subject to a VAT/sales tax (IVA) of either 6 or 12%.

Airport transfer. Bus to the centre of Ibiza Town 85 ptas; taxi from the airport to Ibiza Town or vice versa 1,200 ptas.

Babysitters. 1,000 ptas per hour.

Bicycle and moped hire (per day). Bicycles 700 ptas; moped 1,500 ptas; motorscooters 2,500–4,000 ptas. You will have to pay a deposit.

Buses (one way). Ibiza to: Santa Eulària 150 ptas; Sant Antoni 150 ptas; Sant Miquel 165 ptas.

Camping. 500 ptas per person per day.

Car rental (unlimited mileage). *Fiat Uno:* 4,200 ptas per day, 30,000 ptas per week; *Peugeot 205:* 7,700 ptas per day, 30,000 ptas per week; *Ford Escort:* 9,500 ptas per day, 50,000 ptas per week. Add 15% tax.

Cigarettes. Spanish brands 120–150 ptas per packet of 20, imported brands 200–250 ptas.

Entertainment. Casino 500 ptas (entry is only permitted on production of passport). Discotheque 400–2,000 ptas.

Excursions. Bus tour of Ibiza island 2,800 ptas; Formentera by bus 5,600 ptas; Ibiza Town by night 1,500 ptas.

Hotels (double room with bath in season). 4-star 14,000–19,000 ptas, 3-star 8,000–14,000 ptas, 2-star 4,000–9,000 ptas, 1-star 4,000–6,000 ptas.

Meals and drinks. Continental breakfast 400–750 ptas, lunch or dinner 900–3,500 ptas, beer 125–175 ptas, soft drink 150–200 ptas, Spanish brandy 150–225 ptas, sangría (1 litre jug) 1,000 ptas.

Shopping bag. Bread (500g) 240 ptas, butter (180g) 320 ptas, beef-steak (500g) 800-1,200 ptas, instant coffee (200g) 650-850 ptas, wine (1 litre) 150-400 ptas, fruit juice (1 litre) 150 ptas.

Sports. Golf-green fee 6,000 ptas per day, 28,000 ptas per week. Horseback riding 1,700 ptas per hour. Tennis 1,000 ptas per hour.

Taxi. There are no meters in taxis, but there are legally agreed prices for set journeys, details of which are available from tourist information offices (see page 123).

OPENING HOURS (See also PUBLIC HOLIDAYS on page 121)

Schedules on Ibiza revolve around the siesta, one of the really great Spanish discoveries, aimed at keeping people out of the midday sun. To accommodate the midday pause most shops and offices are open from 9am to 1am and then from 4am to 8am.

Banks generally open from 8:30am to 2am, Monday to Friday, and till 12:30am on Saturday.

Post offices open from 9am to 2am, Monday to Friday, till noon on Saturday. The main office in Ibiza Town keeps longer hours, from 9am to 1:30am and 3 to 8am.

Restaurants start serving lunch about 1am and dinner — earlier here than on the mainland — between 8am and 11am.

PHOTOGRAPHY

Beware of lighting situations you may never before have encountered — especially the blinding reflections from the sea and white buildings. You may not be able to trust the electric eye on your automatic CAMERA in these situations. The secret is to compensate for the reflections with a faster shutter speed.

Most of the popular film brands and sizes are available on Ibiza but they generally cost more than at home. Local shops promise 24- to 48-hour service for both black-and-white and colour processing. The Spanish films, *Negra* and *Valca* in black and white, and *Negra color* in colour, are of good quality and cheaper than the internationally known brands.

For detailed information on how to get the most out of your vacation photographs, purchase a copy of the Berlitz-Nikon GUIDE TO TRAVEL PHOTOGRAPHY (available in the U.K. only).

I'd like a film for this camera.	**Quisiera un carrete para esta máquina.**
a black-and-white film	**un carrete en blanco y negro**
for colour prints	**un carrete en color**
a colour-slide film	**un carrete de diapositivas**
35mm film	**carrete de 35 milímetros**
super-8	**super ocho**
How long will it take to develop (and print) this film?	**¿Cuánto tardará en revelar (y sacar copias de) este carrete?**
May I take a picture?	**¿Puedo sacar una fotografía?**

POLICE *(policía)* (See also EMERGENCIES on page 112)

There are three police forces in Spain. The most famous are the *Guardia Civil* (Civil Guard). Each sizeable town also has its *Policía Municipal* (Municipal Police), dressed in navy blue or uniforms with badges and a blue shirt. The third unit, the *Cuerpo Nacional de Policía* (National Police), a national anti-crime unit, wears a navy blue uniform with a white shirt. All three forces are armed.

If you need police assistance, you can call on any one of the three. Spanish police are efficient, strict, and courteous to foreign visitors.

Where's the nearest police station?	**¿Dónde està la comisaría màs cerna?**

PUBLIC HOLIDAYS

The holidays following are only the national holidays of Spain. There are so many religious, civic, or apparently irrelevant holidays celebrated on Ibiza that nearly every fortnight is bound to include one. It may be only a formality but banks and most shops will close for the day.

With luck, you may be able to help celebrate one of the more colourful local occasions. Since nearly every town is named after a saint, the saint's days take the form of local *fiestas* in the respective places. Ibiza Town lacks a saint's name but not a patron. On 5 August each year, they celebrate the feast day of Our Lady of the Snows. See page 79 for details of some *fiestas* which take place in different parts of Ibiza and Formentera.

January 1	*Año Nuevo*	New Year's Day
January 6	*Reyes (Epifanía)*	Epiphany
March 19	*San José*	St. Joseph's Day
May 1	*Día del Trabajo*	Labour Day
July 25	*Santiago Apóstol*	St. James's Day
August 15	*Asunción*	Assumption
October 12	*Día de la Hispanidad*	Discovery of America Day
November 1	*Todos los Santos*	All Saints' Day
December 6	*Día de la Constitución Española*	Constitution Day
December 25	*Navidad*	Christmas Day
Movable dates:	*Jueves Santo*	Maundy Thursday

Ibiza and Formentera

Viernes Santo	Good Friday
Lunes de Pascua (Catalonia only)	Easter Monday
Corpus Christi	Corpus Christi
Immaculada Concepción	Immaculate Conception (often December 8)

Are you open tomorrow?   **¿Està abierto mañana?**

R

RELIGION

The national religion of Spain is Roman Catholic. On Ibiza, mass is said in no fewer than 33 different Catholic churches, many of them historic edifices. In summer, notices of masses in foreign languages are posted outside major churches in Sant Antoni and Santa Eulària. Protestant services are are also held. Look for notices on hotel bulletin boards. There's no Jewish congregation on Ibiza.

What time is mass/the service?   **¿A qué hora es la misa/el culto?**

Is it in English?   **¿Es en inglés?**

T

TIME DIFFERENCES

Ibiza sets its clocks to Spanish time, which is the same as nearly all countries in western Europe: Greenwich Mean Time plus one hour. In summer, clocks are put one hour ahead (GMT + 2).

Punctuality isn't a Spanish — or Ibicenco — virtue. Only bullfights start on time, because the *toreros* go through agony if delayed.

New York	London	**Ibiza**	Sydney	Auckland
6am	11am	**noon**	8am	10am

What time is it?   **¿Qué hora es?**

TIPPING

Service charge is normally included in your restaurant or hotel bill so tipping is not obligatory. However, it's appropriate to tip bellboys, filling-station attendants, bullfight ushers, etc., for their service.

The chart below gives some suggestions as to what to leave.

Hotel porter, per bag	**minimum 50 ptas**
Maid	**100–200 ptas**
Lavatory attendant	**25–50 ptas**
Waiter	**5–10%**
Taxi driver	**10%**
Hairdresser/barber	**10%**
Tour guide	**10%**

TOILETS (servicios)

There are many expressions for "toilets" in Spanish: *aseos*, *servicios*, *WC*, *water*, and *retretes*; the first two terms are the more common.

Public conveniences are as rare as snowstorms on Ibiza. However, just about every bar and restaurant has a toilet for public use. It would be considered polite to buy a cup of coffee or a glass of wine if you drop in specifically to use the facilities.

Where are the toilets? **¿Dónde estàn los servicios?**

TOURIST INFORMATION OFFICES (oficina de turismo)

Spanish National Tourist Offices are maintained in many countries throughout the world:

British Isles 57–58 St. James's St., London SW1A 1LD; tel. (0171) 499 0901.

U.S.A. 666 Fifth Ave., New York, NY 10103; tel. (212) 265-8822. 8383 Wilshire Boulevard, Suite 960, Beverly Hills, Los Angeles, CA 90211; tel. (213) 658-7188/92.

Canada 2 Bloor St. West, 34th Floor, Toronto, Ont M4W 3E2; tel. (416) 961-3131.

Ibiza and Formentera

These offices can supply you with a wide range of colourful and informative brochures and maps in English on the various towns and regions in Spain, as well as information about accommodation and prices.

Ibiza has a tourist information office at Vara de Rey, 13, Ibiza Town; tel. 30 19 00. It is open from 8:30am to 1pm, Monday to Friday; 8:30am to noon on Saturday.

Where's the tourist office?	**¿Dónde està la oficina de turismo?**

TRANSPORT

Bus services. On Ibiza the bus service hasn't quite caught up with the tourist boom. However, tickets are cheap, and the crowding just might go under the heading of local colour. Private companies link Ibiza with both Sant Antoni and Santa Eulària as well as northern towns. They also operate local runs to beaches. The main lines run a bus every half hour during summer and sometimes extra ones during busy periods. Even so, tourists have been known to miss the last bus. Note that there's no east-west bus service across the island. To get from Sant Antoni to Santa Eulària you must change in Ibiza Town. This jaunt takes about 90 minutes. A hitchhiker could do it in 20 minutes if lucky.

On Formenetera the bus service is irregular and subject to seasonal change; on the whole it is best not to rely on it.

When's the next bus to …?	**¿Cuándo sale el próximo autobús para …?**
single (one way)	**ida**
return (round trip)	**ida y vuelta**

Taxis (*taxi*). The letters *SP* on the front and rear bumpers of a car don't stand for Spain; they mean *servicio pùblico*. The car is a taxi. It may also have a green light in the front window and a taxi sign. Whatever it looks like, it's a reasonably economical mode of transport. Ibiza's taxis have no meters.

The major towns have taxi ranks where the taxis, not the customers, have to queue up most of the time.

What's the fare to …	**¿Cuánto es la tarifa a …?**

Boat services. Ferries link Ibiza with mainland Spain and the south of France (see Travelling to Ibiza on page 126). Getting to Formentera is quick and easy from Ibiza: the 17-km (10½-mile) trip to the port of La Sabina from Ibiza Town takes just over one hour by ferry and 25 minutes by hydrofoil. The journey can be rough, and in adverse conditions the hydrofoils are cancelled. Services are frequent during high season, but reduced at other times. There are also hydrofoil services to Majorca (a 2-hour trip), as well as numerous boat excursions around Ibiza itself that you can find out about on the spot.

The frequency of boat services increases considerably in high season (1 July–30 September). You can get more detailed information by contacting your travel agent.

Hitchhiking (*auto-stop*). In Spain, hitchhiking is permitted everywhere.

Can you give us a lift to …?   **¿Puede llevarnos a …?**

TRAVELLERS with DISABILITIES

Provisions for wheelchair travellers in Spain are not particularly good. There are wheelchair ramps at airports, and many of the larger hotels and apartment complexes also make provision for disabled guests. Some of the more modern resorts provide pavement ramps.

Details of accessible hotels are available from: RADAR, 12 City Forum, 250 City Rd., London, U.K., EC1V 8AF; tel. (0171) 250-3227.

TRAVELLING TO IBIZA

If the choice's of travel to the island are bewildering, the complexity of fares and regulations can be downright stupefying. A reliable travel agent, up-to-date on the latest zigs and zags, can suggest which plan is best.

From the U.K.

By air: All flights to Ibiza's airport are chartered. For direct scheduled flights to Ibiza, travel via Barcelona or Palma de Mallorca.

Ibiza and Formentera

Freedom fares offer savings to those who stay one day to one month, provided you stay over a Saturday night. These fares are ideal if you want to visit several destinations in Spain. Reservations can be changed and stopovers are permitted. **Budget fares** for stays of 1 to 13 weeks in one destination only (no stopovers, no changes in reservations permitted) are available throughout the year. You must travel in and out on the same day of the week. A 50% discount on Budget and Freedom fares is made for children aged 2 through 11. Ask about low "add-on" fares to provincial airports in Great Britain. There are also special low season **money-saver flights** for stays of between one and four weeks (no discount for children).

Fly-drive packages with the use of a car on Ibiza can be obtained with both the Budget and Freedom fares.

Charter flights and package tours (including flight, hotel, and board) are the most popular ways of visiting Ibiza. British travel agents offer guarantees in case of bankruptcy or cancellation by the hotels or airlines. Most recommend insurance, too, for tourists who are forced to cancel because of illness or accident.

By road/car ferry: During the summer, when ferry space is at a premium, be sure you have a firm reservation. The principal routes are: Dover–Calais; Ramsgate–Dunkirk; Newhaven–Dieppe; Weymouth–Cherbourg, Portsmouth–Le Havre, Portsmouth–Cherbourg; and Plymouth–Roscoff. From Ireland, services are Rosslare–Le Havre, Rosslare–Cherbourg; Cork–Le Havre and Cork–Roscoff.

The **hovercraft** from Dover to Calais takes 35–45 minutes and costs only a little more than the ferry, as does the Seacat **catamaran** from Dover to Calais and Folkestone to Boulogne. The route from Paris is entirely toll motorway to Alicante.

There are also long-distance **ferries** between Portsmouth and Bilbao, and Plymouth and Santander (a 24-hour trip). From Santander follow the N623 to Madrid then the N111 to Valencia or Alicante, or the N240 from Santander to Barcelona.

Car ferries link Ibiza with Barcelona and Valencia, as well as with Palma de Mallorca. During the summer months, there are also car-ferry services between Denia and Ibiza and Denia and Formentera, and a weekly ferry between Sète, in the south of France, and Ibiza. Reservations for vehicle space may be difficult in the high season.

By bus: Express coach services run between London and Barcelona and the Costa Blanca, with frequent departures in summer.

By rail: There are two main routes to Spain: via Paris and Barcelona (27 hours) and Paris and Madrid (32 hours). Connections can then be made to Valencia and Alicante. Couchettes and sleepers are available. In addition to the first- and second-class fares, the InterRail Card may be used in Spain by travellers under 26 years of age and the Rail Europ Senior Card by senior citizens. Another fare, the Transalpino, for those under 26 is also a bargain.

Eurailpass: Anyone except residents of Europe can travel on a flat-rate, unlimited mileage ticket valid for first-class rail anywhere in western Europe outside Great Britain. The price depends on whether you want to travel for two weeks or longer, up to three months. Either way, you must sign up before you leave home. **Student-railpass** is the same system but for second-class accommodation. Only full-time students under the age of 26 are eligible.

From North America

By air: Direct daily flights to Madrid, with connections to Ibiza, operate from Miami, New York, and Montreal.

APEX: Return fares can be purchased 7, 14, 21, or 30 days in advance, but flight dates cannot be changed.

PEX: No advance purchase restrictions, but flight dates can't be changed.

Excursion: Return fares, but flight dates cannot be changed.

Economy, Club, First: Subject to no restrictions.

Charter flights and package tours are available through airlines and travel agents. You'll also find charter flights organized by private organizations, companies, or church groups.

The ITX (Inclusive Tour Excursion) lets you book only 7 days ahead for your 7- to 45-day stay. You can pay to extend your stay

Ibiza and Formentera

by up to 45 days. There's also an added fee if you plan additional stops along the way.

WATER *(agua)*

Both still (non-carbonated) and fizzy (carbonated) varieties are available. Water varies enormously in taste and quality, and the bottled variety is good, clean, and cheap.

a bottle of …	**una botella de …**
fizzy mineral water/still spring water	**agua mineral gasificada/agua mineral**
Is this drinking water?	**¿Es esta agua potable?**

WEIGHTS and MEASURES

For fluid and distance measures, see page 110. Spain operates on the metric system.

Weight

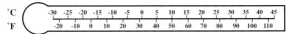

Temperature

Length

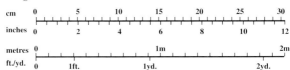

Recommended Hotels

The establishments listed below offer a cross-section of local restaurants, and should convince you that not everything on the island comes with chips (french fries).

The star rating in brackets after each entry refers to the offf-ical government rating system.

As a basic guide, the symbols we use indicate what you can expect to pay for a three-course meal for two, excluding wine, tax and tip. Drinks will add considerably to the final bill.

✪   less than 5,000 ptas.

✪✪   5,000–8,000 ptas.

✪✪✪   more than 8,000 ptas.

IBIZA TOWN

Hostal El Corsario (2 stars) ✪ *Poniente, 5; Tel. 39 32 12; fax 39 19 53.* A characterful, rather Bohemian sort of place, with old Ibizan-style decor, antique fittings and fixtures, and a pleasant terrace. 14 rooms.

Hotel Algarb Fiesta (3 stars) ✪✪ *Playa D'En Bossa; Tel. 30 17 16; fax 30 19 04.* Situated on the beach roughly 3 km (2 miles) from Ibiza Town centre. 408 rooms.

Hotel Torre del Mar (4 stars) ✪✪✪ *Playa D'En Bossa, D.P. 07800; Tel. 30 30 50; fax 30 40 60.* A luxurious hotel on the beach just 1½ km (1 mile) from the town centre, with indoor and outdoor pools, a sauna, and an international-style restaurant. 217 rooms.

Ibiza Playa (3 stars) ✪✪✪ *Playa de Figueretas, Apdo. 18; Tel. 30 28 04; fax 30 69 02.* Pleasant hotel in a scenic spot at Figueretas beach. Garden terrace and swimming pool. 157 rooms.

Mare Nostrum (2 stars) ✪ *Avda. Pedro Matutes Noguera, SN; Tel. 30 26 62.* Large hotel at the beach representing good value at the lower end of the Ibiza price range. With car park, nursery, playground, hairdresser, shops, garden, convention hall, tennis, squash, miniature golf, and swimming pool. 528 rooms.

La Marina (1 star) ✪ *Andenes del Puerto, 4; Tel. 31 01 72.* Renovated in 1991, this is situated directly across from the port.

Los Molinos (4 stars) ✪✪✪ *Ramón Muntaner, 60; Tel. 30 22 50; fax 30 25 04.* Very comfortable hotel occupying a convenient position at Figueretas beach, with a pleasant garden, terrace, and swimming pool on the edge of the sea. 147 rooms.

Montesol (1 star) ✪ *Avenida Vara del Rey, 2; Tel. 31 01 61.* Located in a prime position just on the corner of Vara de Rey, one minute's walk from the port and close to the Dalt Vila. 55 rooms.

Royal Plaza (4 stars) ✪✪✪ *Pedro Francés, 27–29, Apdo. 996 D.P. 07800; Tel. 31 37 11; fax 31 40 95.* Modern hotel just 5 minutes' walk from the port. Rooftop swimming pool with great views of the Dalt Vila. 117 rooms.

Tres Carabelas (3 stars) ✪✪ *Playa D'En Bossa, SN; Tel. 30 24 16.* Popular hotel in a scenic location at the beach and offering all modern conveniences, including swimming pool, tennis courts, gym, sauna, and miniature golf. There is also a garden terrace. 245 rooms.

SANTA EULARIA DEL RIU

ApartHotel Orquídea (3 stars) ✪✪ *Paseo Marítimo, Prolongación D.P. 07840; Tel. 33 14 92; fax 33 19 74.* Modern building on the edge of town and close to the beach.

ApartHotel San Marino (4 stars) ✪✪✪ *Santa Eulalalia D.P. 07840; Tel. 33 03 16; fax 33 90 76.* A relatively recent addition to the Ibiza hotel scene, this is a modern establishment which only opened in 1988. Situated just 60 metres (65½ yards) from the beach, it offers all the facilities you would expect. 44 rooms.

La Cala (3 stars) ✪ *San Jaime, 76; Tel. 33 00 09; fax 33 15 12.* Occupying a central location and offering 180 rooms, including various suites. With a garden and swimming pool.

Hostal Rey (2 stars) ✪ *Calle San José, 17 D.P. 07840; Tel. 33 02 10.* A smaller establishment with 20 rooms, some with sea view. Just behind the Casa Consistorial.

Hotel Cala Nova Playa (3 stars) ✪✪ *Playa Cala Nova; Tel. 33 03 00; fax 33 24 10.* Located 5 km (3 miles) north of Santa Eulària on Cala Nova beach. Full facilities and disco. 305 rooms.

Hotel Don Carlos (3 stars) ✪✪ *Urb. Siesta Apdo. 14 D.P. 07849; Tel. 33 01 28; fax 33 06 34.* On a quiet beach just 2 km (1 mile) from town centre. Many facilities and beach bar. 168 rooms.

Hotel Tres Torres ✪✪ (3 stars) *Junto Puerto Deportivo D.P. 07840; Tel. 33 03 26; fax 33 20 85.* Located at the yacht marina and close to the beach. 112 rooms with modern facilities.

Ses Estaques (3 stars) ✪ *Platja Ses Estaques D.P. 07840; Tel. 33 02 00; fax 33 04 86.* This is a smart and modern four-storey hotel used by package-tour operators, but run with a personal touch by a local husband-and-wife team. 159 rooms.

SANT ANTONI ABAD

Hostal Residencia Florencio (2 stars) ✪ *Rosalía, 38; Tel. 34 07 23.* This *hostal* occupies a convenient location not far from the centre of town. 104 rooms.

Hotel Es Pla (3 stars) ✪ *Avenida Portus Magnus; Tel. 34 11 54; fax 34 04 52.* A large hotel, 170 rooms, with modern facilities, located in pleasant grounds just 200 metres (219 yards) from the beach and 3 minutes' walk from the town.

Hotel March (2 stars) ✪ *Avenida de Portmany, 10; Tel. 34 00 62.* Located close to the Es Pla and Marco Polo but smaller and with fewer facilities. 86 rooms.

Hotel Marco Polo (3 stars) ✪ *Carretera Albiza–Sant Antoni, km 15; Tel. 34 10 50.* This pleasant hotel is located very close to, and owned by the same group as, the Hotel Es Pla. It is a little smaller than its sister establishment, but offers a choice of similar facilities. 107 rooms.

Hotel Milord I (3 stars) ✪✪ *Sant Antoni; Tel. 34 06 12; fax 34 09 66.*

Hotel Milord II Fiesta (4 stars) ✪✪ *Sant Antoni; Tel. 34 12 27; fax 34 09 66.* Hotels Milord I and II stand together in a fairly isolated position across the bay from the town of Sant Antoni. There are two pools, as well as various beaches and a number of other facilities.

Hotel Palmyra (3 stars) ✪✪✪ *Dr. Fleming; Tel. 34 03 54; fax 31 29 64.* This modern hotel is situated in a good location right on the beach and just 1 km (½ mile) from the centre of town. The facilities on offer are above average. 160 rooms.

Hotel San Remo (3 stars) ✪✪ *Bahía de San Antonio; Tel. 34 11 50; fax 34 11 23.* The San Remo is situated on the S'Estanyol beach at Sant Antoni bay, 3 km (2 miles) from the town centre. Many facilities are offered and the hotel caters for children. 147 rooms.

Hotel Tanit (3 stars) ✪✪ *Cala Gracio D.P. 07890; Tel. 34 13 00; fax 34 08 62.* Located just north of Sant Antoni on a peaceful bay. This hotel has many entertainment facilities and caters for children. 386 rooms.

ELSEWHERE ON IBIZA

Hacienda (5 stars) ✪✪✪ *Urb. Na Xamena D.P. 07815; Sant Miquel De Balansat; Tel. 33 45 00; fax 33 45 14.* This is one of the island's most luxurious hotels, stunningly set in a beautiful hillside location and enjoying magnificent views. The decor is traditional and the bedrooms are grand, while the facilities are every bit as impressive as you would expect at the price.

Recommended Restaurants

The establishments listed below offer a cross-section of local restaurants, and should convince you that not everything on the island comes with chips (french fries).

As a basic guide, the symbols we use indicate what you can expect to pay for a three-course meal for two, excluding wine, tax, and tip. Drinks will add considerably to the final bill.

✪	less than 5,000 ptas.
✪✪	5,000–8,000 ptas.
✪✪✪	more than 8,000 ptas.

IBIZA TOWN

Bar-Restaurant Estrella del Mar ✪ *Calle Pedro Francés, 12; Tel. 31 17 80.* Located between the port and the Royal Plaza hotel. Small, basic, with excellent food. Good value *Menu del Día.* Closed Saturday.

Bar San Juan ✪ *Calle Montgrí, 8; Tel. 31 07 63.* An intriguing place where locals mix with tourists. Inexpensive and full of character. Closed Sunday and holidays.

La Masía D'En Sord ✪ *Carretera de San Miguel; Tel. 31 02 28.* A delightful 17th-century farmhouse with romantic outdoor terrace and suitably rustic indoor dining. The huge house is divided into smaller rooms for greater intimacy. Mediterranean cuisine of which the specialities include salmon cooked in *cava.*

El Portalon ✪✪ *Placa des Desamparats, 1-2; Tel. 30 39 01.* Located just inside the old walls (enter by the bridge near the market), this eatery specializes in Spanish and international cuisine, with an emphasis on fish and shellfish.

Restaurante La Brasa ✪✪ *Calle Pere Sala, 3; Tel. 30 12 02.* An unusual place with a lovely garden terrace right underneath the old walls.

Restaurante Formentera ✪✪ *Plaza de la Tertulia, 5; Tel. 31 10 24.* Just across from the port, this restaurant specializes in typical Mediterranean cuisine.

Restaurante La Marina ✪-✪✪ *Andenes del Puerto, 4; Tel. 31 01 72.* Situated right across from the port. Terraces on both sides. 2,500 ptas. per person and a *Menu del Día* at 1,000 ptas.

Restaurante Sa Cocva ✪ *Calle Santa Lucia, 5; no tel.* Difficult to find, but the effort is worthwhile. Inside really is a cave, and the outside terrace has fine views of the cathedral. The menu changes daily. Average price 3,000 ptas. per person.

Restaurante San Telmo ✪✪ *Calle Sa Drassana, 6; Tel. 31 09 22.* Large, impressive, and just inside the maze of narrow walkways across from the port.

S'Oficina ✪✪✪ *Avenida d'España, 6; Tel. 30 00 16; fax 30 32 57.* Located close to the far end of the Vara del Rey and specializing in Basque cuisine, with huge tanks of lobsters and other shellfish. Terrace in summer. Closed Sunday in summer, Saturday and Sunday in winter.

Sa Caldera ✪✪ *Calle Bisbe Pare Huix, 19; Tel. 30 64 16.* Located roughly 5 minutes' walk from the port and specializing in fish and shellfish.

SANTA EULARIA DEL RIU

Ca Na Ribes ✪ *Calle San Jaime, 67; Tel. 33 00 06.* Next to the Celler Ca'n Pere on the main road, and offering a selection of Ibicenco specialities, fish and steak; bar in the garden.

Celler Ca'n Pere ✪✪✪ *Calle San Jaime, 67; Tel. 33 00 56.* The oldest restaurant in Santa Eulària. Delightful environment with fine food and wines.

Restaurante Atenea ✪✪ *Marino Risques, 9.Loal 6; Tel. 33 12 77.* Modern and stylish bar/restaurant located in a central position on the promenade. Breakfast to dinner.

Restaurante Doña Margarita ✪✪ *Paseo Marítimo; Tel. 33 06 55.* A delightful restaurant with views right across the bay. Typically Mediterranean cuisine. Closed on Friday and Saturday in winter and Monday lunchtime in summer.

SANT ANTONI ABAD

Grill Magon ✪✪ *Calle Valencia, 23 Por des Torrent; Tel. 34 02 98.* Serves fresh fish and grilled meats. Closed Monday.

Restaurante Rias Baixas ✪✪ *Calle Ignacio Riquer, 4; Tel. 34 04 84/80.* A little difficult to find, the restaurant is in the old town and specializes in fish cooked in traditional Galician and Basque styles.

Restaurante Sa Capella ✪✪✪ *Carretera Can CGermá, 1/2 km; Tel. 34 00 57.* Just outside Sant Antoni, housed in an old village church. Typically Spanish cuisine; very expensive.

SANTA GERTRUDIS

Bar Cas Costa ✪ *Plaza de la Iglesias; Tel. 19 70 21.* Not strictly a restaurant but not to be missed if you are in the area. Its speciality is sandwiches, and there are numerous hams hanging from the ceiling. Closed Tuesday.

SAN JUAN

Can Call ✪✪✪ *Carretera-San Juan 11, 600; San Lorenzo; Tel. 32 50 55.* Occupying an old farmhouse that has been converted into a restaurant, it serves classical Ibicenco food, has a charming atmosphere, and offers an extensive wine list.

ABOUT BERLITZ

In 1878 Professor Maximilian Berlitz had a revolutionary idea about making language learning accessible and enjoyable. One hundred and twenty years later these same principles are still successfully at work.

For language instruction, translation and interpretation services, cross-cultural training, study abroad programs, and an array of publishing products and additional services, visit any one of our more than 350 Berlitz Centers in over 40 countries.

Please consult your local telephone directory for the Berlitz Center nearest you or visit our web site at http://www.berlitz.com.

Helping the World Communicate